WATER-EFFICIENT GARDENING

WATER-EFFICIENT GARDENING

John Marder

THE CROWOOD PRESS

First published in 2009 by
The Crowood Press Ltd
Ramsbury, Marlborough
Wiltshire SN8 2HR

www.crowood.com

British Library Cataloguing-in-Publication Data
A catalogue record for this book is available from the British Library.

ISBN 978 1 84797 131 9

Illustrations by Caroline Pratt

Typeset by Servis Filmsetting Ltd, Stockport, Cheshire
Printed and bound in Malaysia by Times Offset (M) Sdn Bhd

Contents

Acknowledgements

For allowing me the freedom to walk in and photograph their wonderful gardens, I would like to thank my friends Frances Druce, and Max and Miriam Balme. And for supporting and encouraging me throughout the process, I give very special thanks to my parents, Keith and Marjorie, my wife Swee Lian and sons Ben and Sam. They knew when to tip-toe around me and the word processor. Apologies must go to Snoops who sat patiently by my feet and to the garden outside. It became just a bit too natural that one summer.

Introduction

Water is precious, and if it comes through our taps in a form fit for human consumption, we're very fortunate really in the big scheme of things. Having enough of that special resource to water the plants in our gardens is something we can't always rely on, and perhaps we shouldn't. It may not be restricted through cost or legislation but can become so when demands are high, and splashing it on the garden is just simply wasteful. The massive increase in mains water usage that occurs in England when summer appears is nearly all down to garden watering. It's not been a problem when reservoirs and aquifers have had their fill of winter rain, but that is exactly what did not happen in the winters of 2004–05 and 05–06. So when there was no summer rain to water our gardens and we had to do it ourselves, problems arose leading to feverish outbreaks of hose pipe bans, crispy lawns, gravel beds and subsidized water butts.

Climate change predictions were already at large, and coupled with ambitious plans for building new homes, they struck some concern, if not a mild sense of gloom amongst us upbeat, 'look on the bright side', gardening folk. Diminishing rainfall is expected over the coming decades, with hot dry summers occurring more regularly and greater demands likely made on our scarce water supplies. A more 'Mediterranean' climate may seem appealing to many of us in North Western Europe but it would force change on our gardening habits, not least because torrential rain and extreme winter wetness are also part of the mix.

We're all a bit different in what we want from our gardens, and with variations in soil and local climate, there can be no singular approach to water-efficient gardening. Extremes of weather seem to happen more frequently and weather patterns are clearly becoming more variable, so our ability as gardeners to adapt, and find new solutions, can only increase. Some of the tricks are in engineering: water recycling, storing and pumping it around. But fundamentally the problems we have with gardening have gardening answers and solutions we can apply through the gardening we do. Planning changes, and choosing the plants, planting them and getting them growing, all have big implications on water usage. Plant and soil sciences underpin the methods we have to use water wisely – methods which this book aims to elucidate, equipping the reader with ideas and knowledge to get the most from gardening in these changing times.

RIGHT AND NEXT PAGE: *Extreme weather events. Horsham Park on one day in January 2007.*

CHAPTER 1

The science of water-efficient gardening

THE CRUX OF THE MATTER

Anyone who agrees that a garden needs to have at least some plants in it will recognize its need for water. All living processes that occur in a plant depend on water, and it's also required for taking up nutrients, cooling the plant, and preventing its soft parts from flagging. As gardeners, we want our plants to be productive and healthy looking, which means protecting them from the stress of drought. Water-efficient gardening aims to achieve this, as far as is possible, with water that occurs naturally in the garden. It is based on knowledge and understanding of the journey water takes into the garden, through the soil and the plants, then out again.

Entering by rainfall, snow, sleet and so on, and by the watering we choose to do, some water is held in the soil for plants to take up, but a fair bit is lost as it drains away or evaporates off from the soil surface. Problems occur when the amount of water entering the soil over a period of time is not enough to replace the water taken up by plants and the water which is lost altogether. It is similar to a bank balance, where you're trying to minimize expenditure in order to stay within income. By improving your soil's ability to hold on to rain, and reducing your garden's demand for water, you're less likely to 'fall into the red' and have to supplement your income by watering.

THE ANSWER'S IN THE SOIL

For the water-efficient gardener, the first place to look for potential savings has to be the soil. Reducing water lost, both downwards into the water table and upwards from the soil surface into the atmosphere, represents savings that are sacrifice free. Reducing the garden's need for water, on the other hand, may mean not growing quite what you want, or at least not growing quite so much of it. Although such compromises may sometimes be necessary, it's best to view them as a last resort, and so look first to the soil to ensure it's giving the best that it can.

The natural tendency of a garden to suffer from drought will depend not only on the amount of rainfall and the ability of the soil to absorb and to hold onto that rain, but most importantly on the amount of water that the soil makes available to plants. This available water capacity arises from the fact that a garden soil is actually just like a sponge. It could be absolutely full of water after heavy rain and then a lot of that water would drain away. However, because of its sponginess, there would be a fair amount of water still held in the soil after drainage had stopped. This is the water that plants use, but just as our hands can't squeeze every drop of water from a sponge, there will always be some held so tightly in the soil that roots cannot extract it. Apart from this inaccessible water, the amount the soil holds after drainage is that which is available to plants. It is this that we are trying to increase when we garden in a water-efficient way. To a large extent we can do this, but the inherent quality of the soil we have is most important in determining where we start from.

Soil Texture and Porosity

A good garden soil consists of about 50 per cent solid material, interspersed with pore spaces that make up the remainder of its volume and which make it spongy. Some of the solid component of

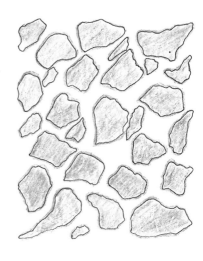

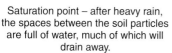

Saturation point – after heavy rain, the spaces between the soil particles are full of water, much of which will drain away.

Field capacity – water still held in the soil after drainage. A lot of this is available to plants.

Wilting point – after plants have taken what water they can, the remainder is held too tightly against the soil particles for them to extract it.

The soil 'sponge' – different amounts of air and water between the soil particles.

the soil is organic matter, but most of it is rock broken down into sand, silt and clay, and it is this that produces the soil texture.

The effects of soil texture on plant growth and on how you garden are many and varied, but they largely arise from the different sized pore spaces that are created by the texture. It is easy to imagine that a dustbin full of cobblestones would have fewer and larger pore spaces than the same sized bin full of gravel. In the same way, because of its larger particles, a sandy soil will have fewer but larger pore spaces than an equal volume of finer textured clay soil.

All this about soil porosity is important because it is within these pore spaces that the soil water is held. As we have seen, if the water is held too tightly or not tightly enough, then plants won't be able to get it. This is determined by the size of the soil pore spaces. The larger pores lose most of their water to gravity, which is essential for ensuring there is air in the soil (*see* page 12). The really tiny pores trap water so plants can't extract it, leaving the middle sized and slightly smaller pores to hold the water that plants use.

Lots of available water is therefore not something that you could expect from either a sandy soil or a clay soil. Rather, it is the loam soils with a wide range of pore sizes and, moreover, many pores in the medium range, that make water most available to plants.

What Kind of Soil Have You Got?

Texture is determined by the relative proportions of the different sizes of rock fragments in the soil. Three different types of particle are identified according to their diameter size range. Sand is the largest (size range 0.06–2.00mm) with clay the smallest (particles below 0.002mm) and silt ranging in size between the largest clay particles and the smallest sands. Clearly the three types of particle cover a wide range, from absolutely miniscule clays to the coarser sands that are something around the size of a match head.

Garden soils consist of a mixture of these three types of particle, and it is the nature of this mixture that determines texture. According to the amounts of sand silt and clay a soil contains, it can

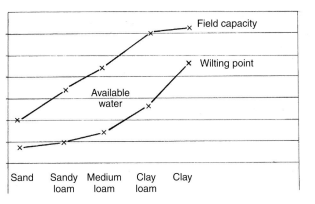

Sand   Sandy   Medium   Clay   Clay
       loam   loam   loam

Diagram showing that loam soils can contain up to three times more available water than sandy or clay soils.

be placed into one of about a dozen textural categories. These range from extreme sands, consisting mainly of sand, to heavy clays or very silty soils. In between are various slightly less extremes such as silty sands and sandy clays and between these is a range of loams with fairly even proportions of the three particle types.

Soil testing for chemical characteristics such as pH and nutrient levels is not possible without some kind of special equipment, but you can obtain information about your soil's texture quite easily by simply playing with a handful of moist soil.

A high proportion of sand will give it a distinct loose and grainy feel while, if it is clayey, a solid ball or worm shape will be easily moulded from it. Lots of silt will make it flake rather than form a worm and it will have a slippery soapy feel instead of the stickiness of clay. If, as you would hope, your soil is a loam, then it will show a combination of these characteristics. For example, a relatively sandy loam would just about form a ball, or a short thick worm, but then would easily fall apart. A clay loam, on the other hand, would form a strong ball or a long thin worm, which would only fall apart if you dangled it from your fingers.

If you've been cultivating your plot already, then you probably won't even need to do any check on texture. You'll know enough, from the experience of digging, how hard the ground is in summer, how sticky in winter, whether you can hear the sshhh! sound of sand grains as the spade pushes through the soil. If it's an unfamiliar plot, then handling the soil as described above will tell you all you need to know. Indeed, for the enthusiasts

amongst us, when looking to buy a new house, a couple of minutes sampling the garden soil would be far more worthwhile than assessing the quality of interior décor. The texture of the soil will influence everything you do in a garden for as long as you're there.

Altering soil texture can be quite involved. It is usually done only for plants that need really free drainage, for which large amounts of sand or grit might be well worth adding. In most cases, however, it will be far more sensible to work with what you have, because normal gardening tasks, such as digging and applying organic mulches, can quickly overcome any problems that arise from soil texture.

The Water Available in Your Soil

For the water-efficient gardener, soil texture is particularly important in influencing the amount of water available from the soil. Clay soils hold a lot of water against gravity, and so are said to have a have a high field capacity. However, they also have a high wilting point because so much of this water is held too tightly against the surface of the particles for plants to extract it. Sandy soils don't have nearly as much surface to hold onto water, so far less is held in the soil that plants can't extract, and their wilting point therefore is low. But their field capacity also is low because they drain so freely and not much is left after drainage is finished. For soils to be able to hold large amounts of available water, they must have a high field capacity and low wilting point – characteristics we find in loamy soils. Not only do loams contain much more available water than the sandy or clayey extremes, but they are able to do this while still providing plant roots with the all-important air they need.

Water and air are essential of course, but there are other important soil qualities that arise from texture too. As compared with a sandy soil, clays stay colder in the spring, delaying seed germination and are far more difficult to cultivate when wet or dry. Although you may curse it when times are bad, clay does however give the soil much better fertility by making essential nutrients far more available to plants. Very silty soils are not common in gardens, but where they do occur they can be a bit like loams in providing a good blend of water retention, drainage and nutrient availability. They can easily suffer problems with poor structure however and so, like sands and clays, benefit enormously from lots of organic matter.

You may have a garden in which the soil is dominated by ingredients other than sand, silt or clay. Very chalky soils are normally free draining and drought prone with low availability of nutrients. Organic matter again is the panacea but that's not the case with peaty soils. They're already full of it because the boggy conditions prevent its complete breakdown. Drought is unlikely to be a problem; quite the opposite but peaty soils can be very infertile so they've often been drained to overcome this.

Improving Your Soil Structure

Of all the things that gardeners may want to know about their soil, those that influence its physical consistency are the most important in making the soil more water efficient. Texture, with its influence on pore space size, is a major aspect of a soil's physical make-up, but the other characteristic important here is soil structure.

Unless you have a really light sandy soil, made up of single grains, the tiny rock fragments that your soil consists of should be joined together into lumps of different shapes and sizes. This soil structure is really important in determining how easily water, air and plant roots can move through the soil, and it can be altered, both for better and for worse, by the way we garden. A good structure will increase the porosity of the soil by providing pore spaces between the lumps. These spaces, although large and therefore subject to water loss, are particularly important in fine textured soils, such as clays, for ensuring the right balance of air and water in the soil. For although we want to hold as much water as we can in the soil, this mustn't be done at the expense of air, which, in providing the oxygen for respiration, is just as important for plants as water is.

Various problems can occur with the structure of your soil. Surface compaction, panning and capping are amongst them and can lead to imbalances in the amounts of air and water your plants get. Careful working of the soil is required, and most important of all – the cornerstone of good gardening practice – is the use of bulky organic matter in its various guises.

There are so many important benefits of organic matter in gardening, many of them to do with soil porosity and therefore important in maximizing the soil's ability to hold both water and air at the same time. It absorbs water, releasing it back to plants, and as it breaks down produces a gluey substance called humus that binds soil particles together into structures. The presence of organic matter in the surface of the soil around plants increases infiltration of water into the soil and, lying on top of the soil, it reduces water loss by evaporation. It provides nutrients for plants, tiny animals and microbes and massively increases the ability of soil to hold onto nutrients.

Without organic matter, soil isn't soil – it's dust. Through decay and decomposition, organic matter comes from the life in the soil, and it puts that life back into the soil, maintaining all aspects of the soil's fertility. The natural cycle of plants living, dying and decaying, and so sustaining the further growth of plants, is part of the magic that is both nature and gardening. Water-efficient gardening has to pay all due respect to this natural cycle in order to gain all the possible benefits from it.

Balance of Air and Water

Plants need air just as much as they need water. Obtaining it is easy for the leaves and stems, but this is not always the case for the roots. Below the ground, availability of air, and the precious oxygen it provides, is dependent on the porosity of the soil. There have to be pore spaces large enough to allow water to drain out of the soil and be replaced by air. By the same token, there have to be smaller pore spaces for holding water and so to provide the crucial balance of these two vital resources in the soil.

In a good well-structured garden soil, you could expect 50 per cent of its volume to be pore space. Ideally for most garden plants 70 per cent of this

WATER PRESSURE AND WILTING

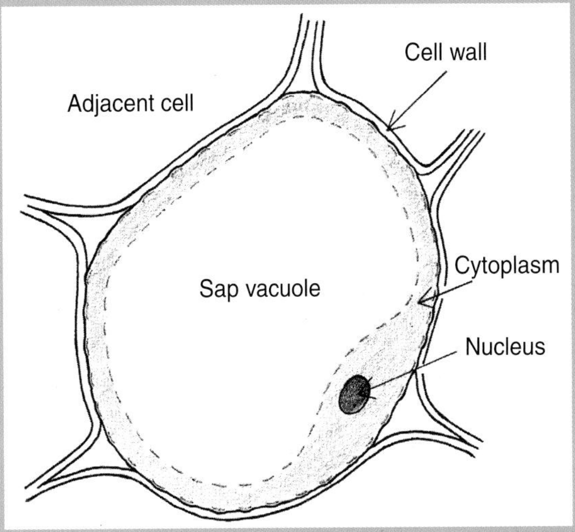

The sap vacuole and cytoplasm in this cell are fully hydrated,
so applying pressure to the inside of the cell wall and keeping the
plant from wilting.

(Diagram labels: Cell wall, Adjacent cell, Sap vacuole, Cytoplasm, Nucleus)

The water in plant cells is held in one or more sap
vacuoles, and in the cytoplasm that surrounds them.
When fully hydrated the vacuoles can occupy more
than 90 per cent of the volume of the cell and, together
with the cytoplasm, they exert a pressure, pushing
against the outer wall of the cell. This wall is fairly
rigid but slightly bendy and, with the pressure pushing against it, the cell becomes pumped up. Millions
of cells together in young plants or any non-woody
tissue, when all pumped up in this way, will hold
the stems firm and upright with the leaves presented
proudly to the sun. Under conditions of drought, the
vacuoles and cytoplasm shrink, causing a slight defla-
tion in each cell, and wilting occurs. If the conditions
persist, the cells become permanently damaged and
the plant dies. If remedied soon enough, however,
the cells get pumped again and you can experience
the great joy of seeing the plant standing proud once
more.

would be filled with water and the remainder air,
but temporary fluctuations, under either very wet
or dry conditions, are of course normal. Prolonged
periods, during which the soil is at, or close to, saturation point, can easily occur in poorly structured
clay soils or in planted containers with inadequate
drainage. Such water saturated conditions, depriv-
ing plant roots of air, can be just as damaging or
fatal as drought, and they are not only caused by
heavy rainfall and poor drainage: well-intended

loving care of favourite container and house plants
can easily lead to death by watering.

WATER JOURNEY FROM SOIL TO PLANT AND BEYOND

Organic matter and soil porosity not only influence
soil water and air, but also have a direct and posi-
tive effect on root development of plants, assisting
them to access the available water.

Water is taken up mainly by the root hairs that
occur just behind the tip of young growing roots.
It enters the root hairs through a process called
osmosis, which is of universal importance in living things. Having entered the root, water finds its
way into the plant's vascular system, where it is
transported up into the stems and then further up
into the leaves.

Approximately 90 per cent of the water that
moves through the plant in this way is lost, dis-
persing into the atmosphere as water vapour. Most
of this passes out through tiny pores (stomata) in
a process known as transpiration. Stomata occur
mainly on the surface of leaves where they make an

Water movement through the plant.

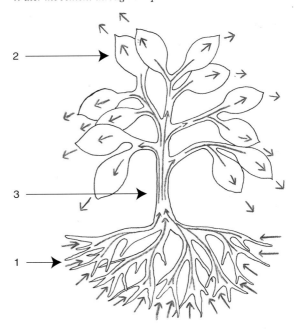

1 Water enters the roots by osmosis.
2 It evaporates from the leaves in transpiration.
3 This draws more water from the roots up the stem to the leaves.

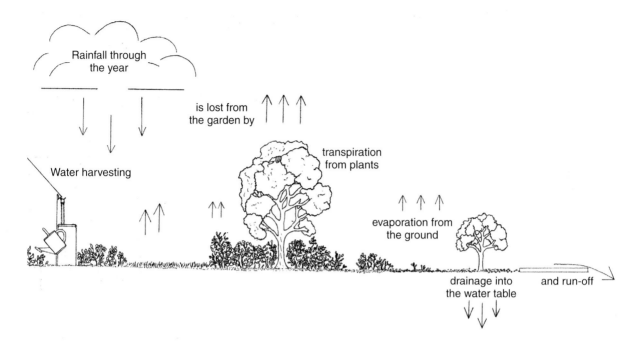

The passage of water in and out of the garden. Over a year the 'ins' balance the 'outs', but in winter, rainfall exceeds evapo-transpiration. That's when loss through drainage occurs. In summer, evapo-transpiration exceeds rainfall; that's when a deficit occurs. Water harvesting compensates for winter losses, so helping you make up the deficit without drawing on water from outside.

important contribution to photosynthesis, exposing the inside of the leaf to the air outside. As a result of this, water in cells within the leaf evaporates off the surfaces of these cells and passes through the stomata into the surrounding air. To replace the water lost, more water moves into the cells and, because water molecules hold together and cling onto surfaces around them, a continuous column of water is drawn up the plant.

The pulling effect of transpiration is immense, drawing water from the extremities of the root system to the uppermost leaves, a distance of well over 100 metres/yards in some large trees. This process epitomizes the unity between the soil we garden on, the plants we grow and the microclimate we garden in. By manipulating this microclimate, gardeners can significantly reduce the rate of transpiration from plants and so reduce the plant's need for water.

The conditions that dry washing on a line are pretty much the same as those that increase the rate of transpiration from plants. Different ways of increasing humidity and shade, or reducing air movement and temperature, can all effectively slow down the rate of transpiration – not forgetting, of course, what we can do to the plant itself, such as removing some leaves. But any reduction in transpiration will involve a negative trade-off: motionless, sticky air encourages fungal diseases. Light, heat and leaves are all necessary for growth.

LIVING WITH LESS WATER

Many plants, through their evolutionary development, have 'chosen' to grow in dry conditions, and so pay the cost of reduced transpiration. In order to avoid living in competition with the vigorous species that grow in wetter places, these extreme drought resistors have developed special adaptations that increase their water uptake as well as reduce their water loss. Reducing water loss compromises photosynthesis, so these plants, known as xerophytes, are generally small and slow growing, but they are able to survive in conditions where most other plants would die. It is as if they've chosen a small winding country road instead of a crowded motorway. Not ideal in some respects but at least there is space for them, and they get there in the end.

Any of our garden plants, whether xerophytes or not, will compromise photosynthesis for the sake of saving water when they need to. This they do by closing their stomata, which may keep them alive, but it is photosynthesis that makes plants bigger. It creates the stuff they're made of, so a well-watered plant is likely to grow much more than one that isn't watered, because it has photosynthesized to its heart's content. The water-efficient gardener, in deciding which plants to water, makes the choice between growth and mere survival. Growing big may be high on the agenda for a cabbage, but for a newly planted shrub, hanging in there until it rains might be enough.

Plants are complex living things with conflicting requirements, as indeed are we. The bigger and lusher the plants we want, the more water they will need and the more they will lose. Getting what we want from our gardens, while reducing the need for water, is the particular conflict we are dealing with here, and understanding the different requirements of plants and soil removes some of the guesswork involved in solving it. The practical solutions described in this book are all, in one way or another, based on understanding of plants and soil, and how water moves through them, between them and beyond them on its way in and out of the garden.

ADAPTATIONS FOR DROUGHT

Large leaves are unusual in xerophytes but those of cardoon are covered in hairs and resourced by deep roots.

Certain plants have become especially adapted to grow in places where drought conditions are common, by having developed characteristics such as these:

- Deep searching roots for seeking and storing water;
- Spreading shallow roots for catching light rain and dew;
- Succulent stems and leaves, allowing storage of moisture;
- Leaves especially modified to reduce transpiration: very small, leathery, waxy or covered in fine hairs, for example;
- Leaves with stomata that open at night rather than in the day, thereby reducing transpiration;
- No leaves at all, with modified stems performing the role of photosynthesis.

Sempervivums are succulents with shallow roots and stomata that open at night.

The various types of rosemary have tiny leathery wilt-free leaves.

The apparent leaves of danae are actually modified stems.

CHAPTER 2

Planning, design and style

Anyone keen to apply their creative flair may not
see garden design as an exercise in problem solving, but that is largely what it is. Whatever mood,
style or purpose you want your garden to have and
whatever features you want it to include or gardening opportunities you want, or don't want, it
to offer, getting it right will involve solving a series
of problems. How to make a shady spot colourful? Where to hang washing so you don't have to
see it? What to do about rabbits? How to combine
privacy with prospect, restfulness with fun, safety
with freedom?

Modern lives are demanding, and present us with
problems. The great designed gardens of history
were the domain of the rich and powerful. With
money no object, and nobody stopping them, solutions were easy. King Nebuchadnezzar II may have
been more water-efficient in his Hanging Gardens
of Babylon had there been no slaves to pump water
from the Euphrates. Ordinary folk of old needed
to grow what they could from the space they had.
With little concern for aesthetics, their commonsense solutions, like terracing and water harvesting,
still stand us in good stead today.

But now there are many things we want from a
garden, and perhaps even more obstacles to achieving them. Good design solutions solve more than
one problem and pull together the different objec-
tives, the overriding aim being to have a garden in
which all components contribute as best they can
to a coherent whole, in terms of both how it looks
and how it functions. In achieving this you need to
set priorities, make compromises and resolve con-
flicts of interest – all of which will most certainly
be involved in designing a water-efficient garden.
Water efficiency, along with all the other things, will
need to be considered at each stage of the process.

PLANNING

Gathering information

The process of design starts with gathering together
information and ideas about the garden site and
how you want to change it. It may be helpful to
use checklists for the site characteristics and the
different garden user requirements, so that nothing
gets missed.

Information about the site will relate largely to
climate and soil. These have a big impact on water
efficiency, as does the house and its potential for
harvesting run-off.

As for the requirements you have of the garden, it may of course not be possible to fulfil them
all. Priorities will have to be set. Water efficiency
would be high on the list, but all feasible requirements should be noted at this stage. Size of garden
and budget are obvious obstacles to achieving the
perfect garden, but the site itself may impose further restrictions. Large trees or buildings blocking
the sun are a case in point. You may just have to
live with them or move house. Shady gardens can
be great to look at, to play and relax in, and water
efficient too. But they don't suit vegetables, greenhouses or stripy lawns. Unless something you want
really won't work, then include it, for now, in your
list of requirements.

What do you want from your garden?
- *Appearance and other sensory qualities*: These are
  usually the most important requirements of
  a garden: its sights, sounds and smells. You'll
  need to think about such things as style, colour
  themes, screening, vantage points, focal points,
  and so on.

- *Fun and relaxation*: You may want it for active things like ball games or children's play, as well as for relaxing and eating outside in sun or shade. Also think about whether you want to create opportunities for gardening or to reduce the need for it.
- *Growing plants*: Of course plants will be important in the look of the garden and how relaxing it is, but you may want, for example, a greenhouse or vegetable area specifically for growing.
- *Practical requirements*: What are your specific needs for storage, clothes drying, recycling and water harvesting? Also consider privacy, shelter, shade and noise reduction.

Assessing your site

- *The microclimate*: Is the garden exposed to strong winds? What is their direction? Are they salt-laden? Is the garden in a frost pocket? Are there frost pockets within it? Which parts will be in sun or shade, in the winter and in the summer? Which parts will be in rain shadow?
- *The soil*: What is the soil texture? Does it vary throughout? What is the soil pH? Does it vary throughout? Is the soil compacted, at the surface

or below? Does it drain well? If not, where? Does it appear to be rich in organic matter?
- *The house*: What is the style of the house? Which way does it face? What microclimates are around it? What materials are used for the house? What colour are they? What are the dimensions of the house? Where are the doors/windows? From where in the house is the garden viewed? What opportunities are there for harvesting water from the house?
- *The garden surrounds*: Is the garden in an urban, suburban or rural setting? Does the setting have distinctive archaeology, geology or ecology? Are there vertebrate pests that could get in the garden? Are there views that need screening out? Are there views that could be used in the design?
- *The garden itself*: What shape is it? What are its dimensions? How level is it? Where are the low bits and high bits? Where are important things (like structures to be retained) located in it? What legal/ownership restrictions are there (like Tree Preservation Orders)? Where is vehicular/pedestrian access to the garden? What opportunities are there for harvesting

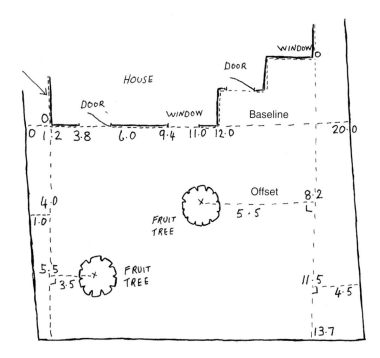

Basic sketch of a garden with the necessary measurements recorded on it. Note running measurements along baselines that are extended from the house, and offset measurements taken at right angles to these baselines

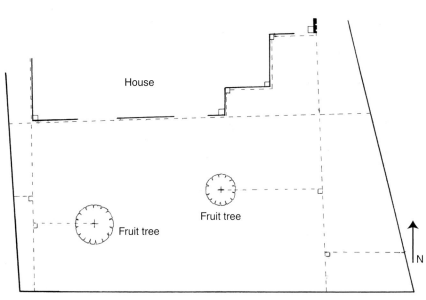

House

Fruit tree

Fruit tree

N

Scale plan drawn from the baseline and offset measurements taken in the previous sketch plan (scale 1 in 200).

water from the garden? What sources of water, such as mains, are in the garden and where are they?

Drawing a plan of the site

An important part of information-gathering is measuring the site, with the purpose of drawing a plan to scale. This might seem unnecessary, but it does help to ensure that your design on paper actually works on the ground. If you're so inclined, computer software could be used to create the scale drawing. Otherwise, a sheet of A2 or A3 paper, a pencil, ruler and set square should do the trick.

The easiest scale is 1 in 100, where 1m on the ground is drawn as 1cm. Before starting to draw, check that your garden dimensions, at the scale you are using, will fit on the paper. If not, get larger paper or use a smaller scale.

Taking measurements

Start by drawing a simple sketch of the garden as you see it, and the part of the house that faces it. You can use this sketch to record your measurements on.

For small gardens with a fairly obvious square or rectangular shape, normal commonsense measuring is fine.

If the area is more complex in shape, or longer than perhaps 15m with particular features such as trees to plot, then some basic surveying techniques may be needed.

Use a tape measure to create baselines along the sides of the house that extend out to the boundaries. Measure the distances along these lines to the boundaries, and record them on your sketch.

A second measuring tape can be used to take off-set measurements from other points on the boundary and anything else that you want to plot, such as trees or the margin of a pond. For the purpose of accuracy, these offsets should meet the baseline at right angles. This is achieved by ensuring that you measure the shortest distance between the point and the baseline. Record the length of the offset and its distance along the baseline.

The scale plan

Only with an accurate plan can you be absolutely sure that everything fits in the place you want it. It acts as the basis for the design.

Start the drawing with the building, or at least the part of the building facing the garden. This is the fixed thing from which everything else has been measured. You can assume its angles are 90 degrees, and draw it to scale using a set square. Then draw the extensions that you measured from it, join up the boundaries and, using the set square again, plot any points measured by offsets.

Designing the garden

Now is the start of the process of putting the garden you want into your scale plan of the site. It's the time for the big decisions about what you can have in the garden and where it will go.

Taking a few steps back to see the big picture first is important at this stage. It enables you to determine the best use for each part of the site without being distracted by details like plants, bricks and statues.

Deciding what goes where

It's tremendously helpful to gather all your ideas into a single image, in the form of a bubble diagram. First make a copy or two of your scale plan (*see* page 19). It helps to have this annotated with comments about soil, microclimate and features to be retained. Be prepared to keep rubbing things out. You might even use paper cut-outs of the prominent features you want to include. Make sure they're at a sensible scale, and just shuffle them around until each is in its optimum position.

Use of space

The division of space is important to consider early on, and for most of us the main space within the garden is that which is viewed from the house. To create an attractive scene here, which draws the eye out into the garden (this is called focalization), you need something with real visual impact – it doesn't matter what, but at this stage you should decide where it goes. It will link the house with the garden, which then becomes an outdoor room.

The uses of this room can then be allocated to different zones within it. Sunny sitting spots, colourful flowery areas, and places for safe play, hidden storage or convenient barbecuing, should all become clear as you stare at your scale drawing and shuffle things around. If the space can be further divided, to form additional garden rooms, that's good – it could provide practical solutions, through separating the different uses, and create refreshing elements of mystery and surprise.

Use of water

Arrangement of space in this way, and how it is used, is always important from the outset, but the particular requirements of a water-efficient garden are a further priority now, while the big picture is in mind.

It may be useful to think of areas as having a high, medium, low or no watering requirement (*see* the bubble diagram on page 21). Most container plantings, annuals and vegetables have a high requirement, needing frequent watering, and should go near the water butts. Perennial borders generally have a medium requirement, needing occasional watering, and so should also be placed near there. Each of these would need moisture retentive but fairly well-drained conditions.

Decorative schemes of drought resistant plants have a low requirement, as do bulkier plantings of trees and shrubs, which may be less needy of sun and good drainage. Plantings like these will rarely need watering, if at all.

A wet boggy area would be good for moisture loving plants, allowing them also a low watering requirement, while for paved areas, with no water needs, such thoughts would be inconsequential – except, that is, if they are used for water harvesting. Juxtaposing a water impermeable hard surface with a sunken bed of moisture loving plants creates the rain garden effect. Run-off from the paving is gratefully received or filters down slowly through the soil.

Levels, surfaces and watery matters

Gentle slopes within a site are fine and attractive, as long as the design uses bold curves that conform with the contours. However, for a formal or geometric design, the ground will have to be levelled, perhaps by constructing retaining walls and sunken areas.

Changing of levels is one activity where as an amateur garden maker you may be stretched beyond your limit. There can be serious consequences to the stability of soil and built structures, drainage and the health of existing trees, so seek help and have the decisions on levels made before proceeding with your design plan.

There are so many different materials available for garden construction and it's worth looking

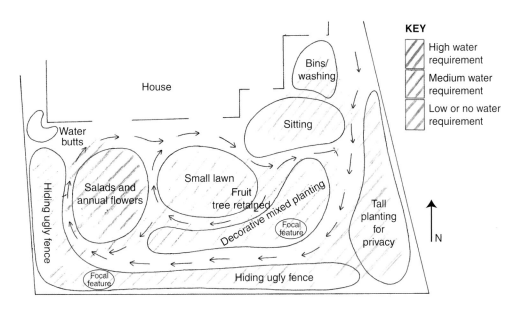

Bubble diagram drawn onto the scale plan, taking into account the known user requirements.

into the full range. They will probably be the most expensive ingredients of your garden, and also carry environmental concerns that you may want to investigate.

One important issue with water is whether it runs off hard surfaces or percolates naturally down to re-charge the water table. Run-off from impermeable surfaces, leading to flash flooding of rivers and water pollution, is quite a problem in urban areas, and it's one that gardeners can help counteract.

Impermeable paving, such as concrete and natural stone flags, can be used to direct run-off into rain gardens – planted beds with a high water demand. Loose aggregates like gravel give good permeability but their use for paving is limited. Normal pavers laid on sand can be fairly permeable, reducing run-off, and special systems have now been developed for constructing hard surfaces with high permeability. These allow direct percolation into the ground or, as can be done with run-off water, carried by pipes to soakaways or catchment tanks.

Rainwater harvesting

Catching rain that lands on your house roof or garden is a big plus in water-efficient gardening, and

harvesting rainwater should be considered at the design stage. The use of water butts attached to down-pipes from the roof is the bare minimum that most of us can manage, but there are various other possibilities that should be investigated.

Rainwater harvesting is essentially anything we do to capture rainwater from where it lands, so we can use it somewhere else and perhaps save it for a less rainy day. It may be as simple as a rain garden (*see* page 154), terraces on a slope (page 134) or even just planting a tree in a bit of a dip where water will run down towards it.

But it's usually something more sophisticated, involving the collection of rainfall from a roof or paved surface and directing it for storage in water butts or underground tanks. If watering is something you'll need to do, then harvesting rainwater is really a must in the water-efficient garden. Plants don't need water that has been expensively treated for human consumption, and where there's a roof there will be run-off, so it may as well be used.

The rain that falls on your roof in a year is probably enough to fill hundreds of water butts, so if you want the kind of garden that needs a lot of water, have as many butts as possible and keep using them. With sheds, greenhouses and garage included, you may have room for one on each drainpipe or even to link several together, allowing overflow from one to the next. Underground tanks hold significantly larger volumes of water, and you can pump it into irrigation systems or to other household uses where water doesn't need to be drinkable.

Then there is also the possibility of recycling water from showers and washbasins. The soaps and shampoos that occur in this 'grey water' are fine for most plants, except those that need acid soil. It can breed germs though, so you shouldn't store it for more than a day if left untreated, and don't use it on edible crops.

There is an immense array of products available for harvesting, recycling, storing, pumping and treating rain and grey water. They can certainly help in making up that summer water deficit (*see* page 14), so are well worth careful consideration.

The garden layout

You can't sit and shuffle bubbles forever, but time spent thinking at this early stage will surely pay back in the finished product where every component of the garden is as effective as it can be.

Your completed bubble diagram shows the approximate location and size of the different garden areas. Now it's time to detail this further in a design plan showing, to scale, the paved areas, borders, lawn and so forth, exactly how you want to mark them out on the ground. This drawing will be your final design plan and, if drawn to a suitably large scale, will enable you to include all the necessary planting details.

In developing the garden layout you will need to think about style, in terms of geometric or curvy outlines, and ensure that the shapes you create fit or flow together into a unified pattern. Proportion and scale are important here, not only from an aesthetic point of view but also for functional reasons. Are paths wide enough and sitting areas big enough? The third dimension of height, of course, must not be forgotten, and here you will be considering other qualities such as space and balance.

You also, at this stage, must consider the plants and other materials that you want to be using. Not all paving materials are suited to curvy outlines, and

it's best not to have to cut slabs so they do need to fit the allotted area. Narrow slithers of lawn or the ends of beds tapered to slender shapes might look all right on the drawing, but they can be a problem when it comes to fitting in plants or the mower. Ease of maintenance must be considered when you get down to these details, and hacking back plants that grow over a path or lawn can deprive them completely of all their charm.

Choosing the plants

For keen gardeners, this is the fun bit. Hopefully you will have resisted giving it too much attention up until now, for not seeing the wood for the trees, or the garden for the plants, can be a problem. The areas of planting, and the positions of larger plants, will be shown on your design plan. You may well have had various thoughts about the nature and appearance of the planting, with examples of plants that you might include, but now it's time to get down to specifics.

Balancing conditions and style

The growing conditions that plants require need considering alongside any thoughts you have about form, texture, colour, size, season of display, and whether the plants should be deciduous or evergreen. Cost, availability and maintenance requirements will also come into it, so there is a lot to think about. There are so many plants to choose from, and it's easier when you can narrow the list down early. This happens anyway if the conditions you're choosing for are particularly difficult, such as really clayey or rabbit infested. Otherwise, you can draw up your own list of favourite plants, and then work from that, remembering all the time your site conditions and your desired effect.

Colour themes and notions of style and character can help unify planting schemes as well as focus your mind when choosing the plants. There are those of us who like our plants to be tight and compact with a clearly defined shape, those that like a more shaggy look and others who like a bit of both. It's not quite like choosing a hairstyle or a puppy, but if you know what you want, you can disregard the rest and you're halfway there.

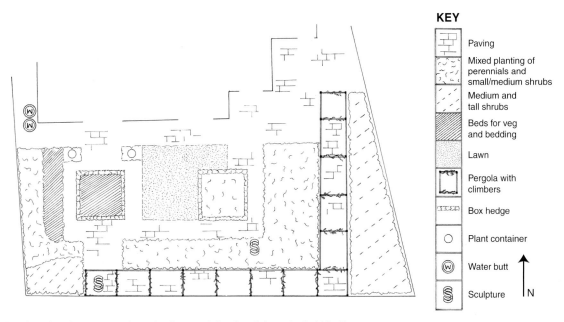

KEY

	Paving
	Mixed planting of perennials and small/medium shrubs
	Medium and tall shrubs
	Beds for veg and bedding
	Lawn
	Pergola with climbers
	Box hedge
○	Plant container
Ⓦ	Water butt
Ⓢ	Sculpture

Final design plan drawn onto the scale plan, and developed from the bubble diagram.

Where to go and what to get?

Often the most useful way of narrowing down your range of plants is to use the current availability lists of one or two nurseries that you know and trust. Searching high and low for this plant or that can be bothersome. It's well worth doing if your heart is set on something particular but certainly not the trouble free option if you just want a nice garden. Plants that you see regularly in your area, and that are readily available, are probably easier to grow than rare connoisseur's plants that are hard to get. It comes back to whether you want a garden for growing plants or an outdoor room. The effort to find and then nurture a plant only to see it fail is sometimes the painful price you pay for the fun of gardening. For others who seek their thrills elsewhere, simpler solutions are required.

Beware of really easy options though. A trip to the garden centre on a sunny spring bank holiday, and picking out all that takes your fancy, is never a good idea when you're looking to plant whole areas of the garden. Like doing the weekly shop when you're really hungry, impulse buying can mean bad choices, giving you a garden that only really looks nice in May or, even worse, one full of miserable plants.

Also important to avoid is the 'one of everything' approach that might have seemed helpful when you last bought fireworks. Planting in groups works best for many plants, and repeating plants throughout the garden mimics the way they occur in nature and helps give that sense of mutual belonging.

Does it need water?

Gardening with zero or minimal irrigation is challenging, whether you're growing unusual plants or sticking to the more reliable ones. Plant selection to suit your conditions is essential. A happy plant will be self-reliant and able to find its own water. Sunny or shady, sheltered or exposed, acid or alkaline, dry or wet – above all else, you need to be as sure as you can that the plant will like it there. A hydrophyte with big lush leaves won't like a dry sandy soil, but a leathery-leaved or succulent xerophyte in a heavy wet soil will be just as unhappy. It not only tolerates dry conditions but depends on them.

Free-draining raised beds and lots of grit could create the dryness for xerophytes, but unless you've set your heart on those kinds of plants, it would be best to use the water that nature provides, and not have it drain away. Heavy clay soils, waterlogged in winter and bone dry in summer, are always difficult conditions to choose plants for. Well-timed cultivations and lots organic matter (*see* page 12) will be a part of the solution, but the rest is down to correct plant choice. This is what brings the rewards, whether it's with a bit of geranium from next door or a rare gentian from the floral marquee at Chelsea. If you can give it the right soil and microclimate, a little bit of help to get going, protect it from being smothered or eaten, then it should get by on minimal fuss.

A common sense, no fuss approach is always good. If you've got extreme soil conditions you'll need to choose extreme plants. If you haven't, you won't, which means there's a wide range of plants at your beck and call. Having said that, extreme climatic conditions are becoming more common, and hot dry summers can ruin green flowery gardens. Annuals, perennials and lawns are particularly at risk, so it makes sense to choose with care. Some species are more tolerant of drought than others, as are certain varieties of those species. This is particularly the case since the attention of plant breeders has become more focused on drought resistance.

Plant adaptations to drought are fairly apparent when looking at plants, so if you're not sure about a plant's tolerance, you can make a judgement based on the size and surface of its leaves. The harder it is to imagine the leaves wilting, the more drought-resistant the plant is likely to be.

The key plants that you're choosing for focal points, dividing space, creating balance and so on, are ones you really want to rely on. These are also the plants you should choose first, before working down to the smaller shrubs and perennials that will make up your decorative beds and borders. If you're taking risks with plants you're not sure about, as inevitably you will sometimes, then do this with the little incidental plants that don't affect your overall plan.

Placing the plants

As you start to look at the finer details, choosing plants becomes closely tied in with their arrangement and spacing. How many you need, and how closely planted, will depend on the plants you choose – not only on their names but also the size of the plants you buy.

The 'big picture' principle still applies, so choose the larger plants first. These will give the bed its 'all year round' structure and focal emphasis as well as fulfilling any need for screening, privacy or shelter. Small trees and large shrubs will normally be planted as individuals, or possibly in groups of three, in key locations to create this framework to the planting. Medium sized shrubs, which grow up to around eye level, can then be selected and positioned. Tall grasses that stand through the winter have the same presence as these so could be used instead. Finally you can include the smaller shrubs, perennials, grasses, bulbs and so on that will give a lot of the sparkle and seasonal variation.

Generally with the smaller plants, the tendency to place them in groups becomes greater, and the spacing between plants becomes closer. Try to imagine how it will look, perhaps by sketching a side-on view, and don't be too apprehensive. It's your garden so there's nothing to stop you moving things around in the year after planting, even if it means a bit more watering to get things going again.

Detailed design of a bed or border

Your decision about one plant goes on to influence further choices as you get into the detailed design of a bed or border. If you love plants, this is worth doing yourself, simply for the fun you'll have and for the knowledge you'll gain about the plants you're using. It's an intricate process though, and if your main priority is just getting it done, it may be useful to have someone to help you.

You'll need a list of plants you want to include, and a base plan of the bed or border you want to plant. An ideal scale is 1 in 50, so if your design plan was done at a smaller scale (e.g. 1 in 100), you will need to do another drawing of the specific planting area.

Bearing in mind the spread of the plants (see page 38), and drawing them to scale, place the larger plants first. Smaller plants, below eye level, are usually best placed in groups of say 3, 5 or 7 at fairly closely spacing. For example, perennials to shin height may be 40cm (16in) apart, knee height 50cm (20in), waist height 60cm (24in) and head height perhaps 75cm (30in) apart. These can drift in front of, and amongst, the larger shrubs and trees.

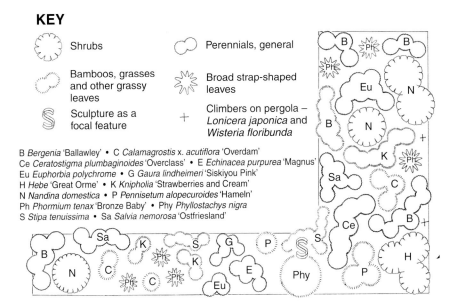

KEY

- Shrubs
- Perennials, general
- Bamboos, grasses and other grassy leaves
- Broad strap-shaped leaves
- Sculpture as a focal feature
- + Climbers on pergola – *Lonicera japonica* and *Wisteria floribunda*

B *Bergenia* 'Ballawley' • C *Calamagrostis* x. *acutiflora* 'Overdam'
Ce *Ceratostigma plumbaginoides* 'Overclass' • E *Echinacea purpurea* 'Magnus'
Eu *Euphorbia polychrome* • G *Gaura lindheimeri* 'Siskiyou Pink'
H *Hebe* 'Great Orme' • K *Knipholia* 'Strawberries and Cream'
N *Nandina domestica* • P *Pennisetum alopecuroides* 'Hameln'
Ph *Phormium tenax* 'Bronze Baby' • Phy *Phyllostachys nigra*
S *Stipa tenuissima* • Sa *Salvia nemorosa* 'Ostfriesland'

Planting design for one of the beds shown in the final design plan (see page 23). The bed consists primarily of low-growing grasses and other perennials in groups. A bamboo and sculpture provide a focal point as viewed from the sitting area by the house, and climbers on the pergola at the back provide height. The planting fits into the zone of medium water requirement because some of the plants may need watering in summer after about three weeks with no rain. (Scale 1 in 100.)

The plants you can buy

When you buy nursery stock, you can often get the same plants in different sizes, and the choices you make have important implications on cost, spacing and ease of establishment. The key benefit of going for the larger plants is the quicker effect they give. However, aside from cost, the key disadvantage is that more care is needed to get them growing. In particular, the water demands of larger plants in the first couple of years after planting are high. This is because their root systems are small in relation to their tops. The relatively low root:shoot ratio means that it is more difficult for the plant to supply itself with water, so all the more help it will need from us. Whether bare-root, root-balled or container grown, anything that is newly planted will have trouble with water uptake because its root growth is restricted and doesn't explore the surrounding soil. The bigger the plant, the greater the problem, so the water-efficient approach is to use younger, smaller plants as much as possible.

Plants twice the size are normally much more than double the price, though in many cases planting larger means you can space them further apart and use fewer of them. Transportation of larger plants is more difficult, and special equipment may be needed to plant them. Perhaps most importantly, when you plant for instant effect, you don't get the satisfaction of seeing things grow quite like you do when you plant small. If there are no existing plants being retained when you plant a new garden, then perhaps just plant some of the key specimens as larger stock to give an air of maturity from the outset. Indeed, if you have any seriously destructive influences in your garden, like a large bouncy puppy, thriving bunny populations, or regular football matches, then you may find large plants are more likely to withstand the onslaught. Certainly when planting out annuals, vegetables and perennials, the larger the plant, the more chance it will have of surviving slugs.

Price is a significant factor in choosing which size to get, and it depends of course on how many you're buying. A transplant for hedging may be about the price of a loaf of bread, while a feathered tree for a small grove in a wildlife garden could be ten times that. A heavy standard planted as a specimen could be ten times again, and then add a further nought still for a large semi-mature tree.

Herbaceous perennials and shrubs are normally sold in container sizes of 2–3 litres (½–1gal) or upwards, with larger specimen shrubs available in much larger containers.

Bare-root, root-balled or container-grown?

Most plants nowadays are grown in containers because it means they can be sold all year round. The alternative is that they're grown in the field, but these can only be dug up and sold in the dormant season. Field grown plants are sold bare-rooted, that is, cleaned of all soil, or root-balled where they're dug up more carefully with the soil retained around their roots.

The production of container-grown plants is far more water demanding than growing in the field. If you plant them in the summer, you'll be using much more water too. All things considered, bare-root deciduous plants lifted and sold after leaf fall in winter is a sensible approach, but be warned and handle with care. The roots must never dry out, and if the plants are big, results can be disappointing. The root:shoot ratio can be very low, placing high demands on water in the first year.

Keeping design in perspective

Garden design doesn't have to be a deliberate 'one-off' paper exercise culminating in a sudden makeover that completely transforms almost everything about a site. It can happen over time in a more instinctive way, without any thoughts of surveys, drawings, plant lists or budgets, and the changes implemented in stages, as time and money allow. Indeed, many beautiful gardens have evolved in this way through the loving, careful and considered endeavours of a gardener. That person would have a clear intent for the garden, and perhaps a visual image in their mind, but would be always willing to experiment and change things, as they strive, over time, to realize that vision.

Even if this approach seems to suit you better, it is still helpful to understand the deliberate process of design. All of its stages, from getting to know the site, through the spatial arrangement of different components, to the selection of plants, will need to be considered at some point, no matter how the garden is developed.

Of course when a garden is designed and made in one go, it rarely stops there. Plants grow, minds change and the garden evolves.

In a gardener's garden, where plants prevail, the decisions made when pruning and thinning can contribute just as much to the 'design' as does an armchair exercise like selecting and ordering plants. If you see the garden as a room for living outside, rather than a place for gardening, you'll

---

SIZES OF NURSERY STOCK TREES

Semi-mature: These are about 4m tall and upwards with a girth (circumference at 1 m above ground) of 20cm (8in)+. They are sold root-balled or in containers of 85 litres (25gal) volume or more.

Heavy Standards and Advanced Nursery Stock: These are about 3.5–5m/yd tall and 12–18cm (5–7in) in girth. They are sold root-balled or in containers of 45 litres (10gal) or more.

Standards: These are 2.5–3.5m/yd tall with a girth of 6–12cm (2½–5in). These are typically in containers of 15 litres or more but may be root-balled or bare-root.

Feathered trees: These have side shoots all the way down the stem and are normally about 1.5–2.5m/yd tall.

Whips and transplants: These are smaller stock, about 40cm–1.5m (15in–1½yd), that are available for species bought in large quantities, like hedging. They are typically bare-root or in small deep containers.

Field-grown evergreens need to be root-balled.

still need to consider maintenance when designing it, and continue to review the design while maintaining it. This is no less the case with the water-efficient garden. The planning, implementation and maintenance are all interlinked, and water efficiency, along with other qualities, will depend on all three.

Good design is important but it's not the 'be all and end all', despite the impression we get from garden shows, television and glossy magazines. Lifestyle images of 'designer' gardens can guide and inspire, but ultimately, whether you sit down and plan your garden or have it unfold around you, the joy will come from your day-to-day life in it, whatever the style.

STYLE

You probably have some idea of the kind of garden you want, how it should look and the kind of character it should have. Such ideas have probably become firmer intentions in the process of thinking about your needs, and no doubt took on a slightly more tangible form when you drew a plan.

You may want it to look contemporary or not, natural or not, but whatever kind of garden you like, it will be the personal stamp that you put on it that will make it fit into the space you have and the life you lead. Design and gardening have to come together in a way that suits you. For some, the main pleasure of the garden comes from the picture created and the peaceful ambience. For others, it comes from collecting and growing plants, while attracting wildlife and producing food may also be strong incentives. But confused you need not be; your own personality and interests will find their way through the choices to arrive at a style that sits easy with you.

The natural look?

Most of us would agree that beauty can be found in nature and that it can also be artistically constructed. In designing a garden we are drawing on nature as well as our own creativity. You may want your garden to express your creative spirit in a very obvious way, or you may prefer it to look like something from nature. Most of our gardens come somewhere between, but the placing of emphasis on one or the other, and the options for blending, are best considered at an early stage.

The truly wild or natural looking garden will hopefully not look designed at all. Native and wild plants are cleverly used to create the effect of a woodland glade, beautiful in its natural simplicity. Such gardens are easy to look after and are great places for children to play and learn.

If you're keen on the natural look but want it to be more of a garden than a wild place, then you can combine a wide range of exotic plants, choosing them for their decorative qualities to create a 'naturalistic' garden. Don't worry, you'd still have the option of wearing clothes. It's just that the garden, though clearly designed, would mimic the rhythms and patterns of natural places like flowery grassland, heaths, woodland and pond margins. A love for plants, and passion for learning, are what you'd need to make such a garden, but you could take a really relaxed approach to its upkeep. Plants can die and self-seed, and weeds can grow here and there, without seriously spoiling the effect. Minimal pruning and weeding would be required, and there would be hardly any need for feeding, spraying or watering. This approach of 'growing hard' relies on selecting plants that suit the conditions more than anything, and makes a perfect water-efficient garden for those who love the natural look of hardy plants.

For a slightly more manicured garden, perhaps with seasonal plantings, containers, nice lawns and a generally more 'gardeny' look, you could adopt the informal approach most frequently seen today. There is no clear attempt to make the garden look natural, but the artificiality of geometric shapes and symmetry is avoided, and the appeal of the garden would still lie primarily in the natural beauty of its plants. This holds true too with most formal gardens, though symmetry, straight lines and geometry do figure strongly in their layout and structure. Plants may be trimmed into all sorts of shapes or arranged in rows to look all but natural, but not necessarily so.

In contemporary engineered gardens, heavy use of artificial materials, such as steel, glass, concrete and graded aggregates, seems to represent the

Hart's tongue fern on a wild shady bank.

Naturalistic planting – loose and scruffy, but growing hard.

It's only natural – forget-me-not and bronze fennel self-seed.

opposite extreme to the wild garden. If your site is big enough, it will allow you to grade from hard and constructed at one end to completely wild and woolly at the other, bearing in mind that there will only be so much garden that you will be able to care for intensively.

The extremes of the engineered and wild gardens require very little in terms of general care and watering. The low maintenance and water-efficient credentials of naturalistic plantings have already been highlighted (see page 28), so it's the conventional garden plantings of all those things we want to grow that need the most of our time and water. If this causes concern, then avoiding really formal designs can lessen the pressure. Anything planted for symmetry, uniformity or in straight lines, needs to grow well or else! Everything has to be in order or it's out of order. Planting informally in drifts not only gives a more relaxed look but will allow you to relax more too. When there's only enough water for your containers and vegetables, and you have to cut down a few wilted perennials or shrubs in a border, hopefully it will only be you and the slugs who know.

Which style?

The garden you have in your mind's eye might have a particular style, such as Mediterranean, Japanese,

English cottage or tropical, or might even be a blend of styles.

Mediterranean garden

The terms, 'dry garden' and 'Mediterranean garden' are almost synonymous in today's garden speak. This is fair enough when you consider the hot dry summers with which Mediterranean gardens contend and that the native plants of the region, adapted to those conditions, are prime candidates for the dry garden. Similar drought tolerant plants also occur in other parts of the world where the Mediterranean climate exists. Recognized by ecologists as a distinct biome, on a par with tropical rainforest and tundra, this scrubby xerophytic

Smart but casual – robinia, phormium and box feature in elegant formality at The Burrows, Debyshire.

Planting softens the formal framework at Horsham museum.

vegetation (see page 15) also occurs as Californian chaparral, as well as south of the equator in Chile, Southern Africa and South Western Australia.

Just like wine merlots and chardonnays, the plants from these places share certain fundamental characteristics but not the names on their labels. Evolving in isolation, different species in different continents have adapted to similar conditions in the same sort of ways. Whether Californian lilac, Spanish broom or dwarf Australian eucalypts, a wide range of tough, slow-growing shrubs form the familiar face of this Mediterranean vegetation, wherever it occurs. Often leathery leaved, spiny or aromatic, growing here and there over open sun-baked stony slopes, they create the permanent look, illuminated seasonally by flowering bulbs that lay dormant through the long hot summer.

One kind of Mediterranean garden is the naturalistic one, copying and jazzing up the wild stereotype and combining suitable looking plants from any of the regions and beyond. Phormiums and hebes from New Zealand, yuccas from Carolina and bottlebrushes from New South Wales, may not be strictly Mediterranean, but then nor is our weather. Many Southern Hemisphere species are not winter hardy for most of us, but there are plenty of plants with the Mediterranean look that love the free drainage you need to provide and remain in keeping with the natural effect.

It has to be said, though, that looking natural has never been a priority in the garden traditions of Mediterranean countries. The Italianate style is classically formal, with shades of green and stone greys prevailing and flower colour only incidental – elegant in its simplicity, but not sitting comfortably with a discarded dog's bone or plastic football, and then there's the need for uniform growth and zero losses if you want perfect symmetry.

Another option for formal design is to gain inspiration from French country gardens. Symmetrical beds, edged with box or lavender, and planted inside with an abundance of things to eat and to look at. This potager style has much to offer if you like home-grown food and the fun of gardening. You may well be out there all weekend though, and you'll need as many water butts as there is room for.

Far less demanding on your time or your water is the Mediterranean courtyard style: the classic dry garden, a room outside where the plants and people sit back and let it happen. Nothing too manicured, but just a stylish relaxing space with large terracotta pots, vine-covered timberwork and some nice 'Mediterranean looking' plants.

Japanese garden

Another great tradition of dry gardens, but the Japanese garden arises from the ancient roots of garden art, rather than from the constraints of climate and soil. Japan is really quite a rainy place, with the same type of natural vegetation as Western Europe and the eastern side of North America.

The Italian Garden at The Burrows, in Derbyshire.

This deciduous woodland biome is characterized by the familiar broadleaved trees and herbaceous perennials of our countryside and gardens, plants that grow so lavish and lush in the wet warm summers that they can afford to close down completely in the winter. Of course there are evergreens too, particularly from under the woodland canopy, making the most of light that shines through the bare winter branches. So many of the plants that we grow in the West come from Japan or similar climates in China, and often they are direct counterparts of our own native species: maple, holly, geranium and so on. The actual species may differ, but the general demeanour of the natural vegetation is the same both West and East.

This cannot be said of the gardens though; similar plants are used in completely different ways. The various styles of Japanese garden are all unmistakably oriental with a distinctive quality that has its roots in a deep veneration of nature. Wonderful scenery is represented in miniature using symbolic garden imagery. Rocks and small groups of plants become mountains and forests, with lakes and rivers of raked sand, hence the dry gardens – dry in appearance and in their water demands. The simplest, most extreme, of these minimalist 'Zen gardens' can have no plants at all. If there are plants, they are used, as with the rocks, very sparingly. Uncluttered emptiness, in the form of sand, is essential to the neat composition that is the essence of these gardens. They are pictures to look at though, rather than places to walk and roll around in – a clear-cut case of right lifestyle, right garden.

Mediterranean courtyard style at the Horsham home of garden designer Stephen Morphew.

More liveable in is the tea garden style, which brings with it the bits and pieces of the Japanese garden: stone lanterns, water basins, little bridges and Buddhas, but consult a friend with good taste before getting carried away. Tea gardens are essentially simple and naturalistic, with dappled shade, mosses, ferns and a wonderful 'sense of place' – a quality most apparent when the garden is wet with rain, so it's customary, when necessary, to damp it down for appearance's sake. Water wisdom has probably never been high on the agenda of Japanese gardeners, but then Japanese gardens are not particularly water demanding. Planting is minimal. There is little or no seasonal display that needs renewing, and plants are chosen to suit the conditions. If you want a dry garden but don't have the sunny free-draining site you'd need for a Mediterranean one, then gravel and stones with a Japanese twist could be the answer.

English cottage garden

Over the centuries, while wealthy landowners have pursued the comings and goings of garden fashion, ordinary people have passed on their gardens and gardening craft to the next generation. Free from the various influences that underpinned landscape changes on big estates, the cottage gardens of country people evolved only very slowly. If there was space around to grow things then that is what they did, and that space would have been used to its full potential. Their livelihoods depended on maximum gain from a small piece of land: fruits, vegetables, herbs and flowers too, to sell by the road and aid pollination. But as time went on, there became less need to grow things for use, so there was more time and space for growing for fun, hence the really flowery English cottage garden, known and loved worldwide. From its humble roots it had become a design style, adapted to all sorts of not so humble, and not so rural, properties.

If you think it suits you and your site, though, beware of over-designing. The charm of the cottage garden is in its 'what you see is what you get' earthiness, not trying to be anything more than an area around a house where someone loves to grow plants for all the good things they offer.

Primarily summer gardens, with herbaceous perennials and annuals, you may want to think about evergreen hedges and shrubs to get some winter structure. Lawns are not really part of the picture. Cottagers of old would have had neither space to waste on them nor mowers to cut them. Paths, of brick or stone, are best kept straight, in a 'no nonsense' sort of way, but the busy planting, and lack of pretentiousness, keep it all very informal.

Stephen Morphew's Japanese tea garden.

Contemporary favourites, like grasses and palms, don't fit well but you don't have to stick to the old cottage stalwarts. Flowers in abundance are what you need with a little thought spared for height, colour and season. But not too much; carefully themed borders would look too designed. It's all about the plants and the growing of them. A cottage garden is a real gardener's garden so you'd have to be up for it – sowing annuals, staking perennials, pruning climbers, making compost; it's not just a nice design idea, but almost a way of life for those with the time and the passion.

'Tropical' garden

Well that's one name for it, capturing the spirit of abundant growth with an exotic 'jungley' look. Foliage prevails, and plenty of it, as large and lush as it can grow. If you don't mind the work – moving plants indoors and out and wrapping them up – then you can really go to town on the tropical theme. If you want your jungle to look after itself

Cottagey planting at the Horsham museum.

most of the time, then you'd have to stick to more familiar hardy plants but those with a real tropical look. In either case, a framework of hardy evergreen shrubs and bamboos is a good starting point. It gives solid winter structure and the tall growth

Foxgloves and alliums at Copyhold Hollow, West Sussex.

you need for a mini jungle. Any less hardy plants can snuggle up amongst them, lessening the need for your mollycoddling.

In the tropical garden there are leaves everywhere – on the ground, in the canopy, halfway between and climbing over the top. A good fertile loam is what's needed for all this growth, and good drainage will reduce the impact of winter frost on many plants that are only just hardy. Getting chilled to the bone is one thing, but drenched to the core at the same time is a bit too much. During the warm growing months however, many tropical plants and their hardier look-alikes can really lap up water. Keeping the tender plants out of the frost will, in itself, make further demands. Growing in containers for moving under glass, and planting into beds in May or June, are both fairly water extravagant things to do, so tropical gardens are definitely not dry gardens. Their very nature is the 'land of plenty', and that includes the precious liquid. Growing things close together and putting containers under the shade of taller plants do, however, start to make water-efficient sense. Then with the right plant selection, good soil care and resisting the lure to plant it all fully grown out of dustbin sized pots, your water-efficient jungle becomes quite feasible. You can relax in the wonderful cooling and shade that the plants offer, and if you're growing the tender ones, save your gardening time for the big autumn cover up.

Design elements

Form, texture and colour

These are the key visual qualities that you should think about when choosing and combining plants and materials in your garden. *Form* is the outline shape of things. It could be artificial shapes like sculptures or topiary, or it could be the more natural shape of plants. Many cultivars have been developed for their distinctive upright, weeping or horizontal forms which do not represent the way that species looks in nature. These plants can be good for creating points of interest, but you should use them sparingly if you want the garden to have a natural feel.

Some leaves are so big and bold that they form the outline of the plant, but for most plants, the

Eriobotrya, phormiums and cordyline in jungley planting at Horsham Park.

leaf size and shape are what gives the effect of *texture*. This can range from the very fine and feathery appearance of plants with small leaves or leaflets to the more bold and chunky appearance of plants with large, broad or strap shaped leaves. These effects of fineness and chunkiness are accentuated if the leaves are widely spaced and don't overlap so much. Construction materials like fine gravels and chunky cobbles have similar textural effects that combine well, in different ways, with both plant texture and form.

Combinations of stones and rocks with sparsely placed plants are characteristic of naturally arid landscapes and are often mimicked when creating dry gardens. In adapting to dryness, xerophytes

Form, texture and subtle tones from hebe, eucalyptus and phormium.

have modified their overall size and shape, as well as the size and shape of their leaves. The reduction in leafiness gives them a certain texture, but there are particular shapes also that feature strongly amongst xerophytes.

Plants in dry landscapes are often quite far apart, because the soil can't support dense lush growth. This isolation not only moulds the shape of the plants but also gives visual accent to it, so form is particularly important in the design of dry gardens. Receiving light from all around, xerophytes are generally clothed to the ground with foliage, and the cover this creates over the soil surface acts like a living mulch, conserving the precious water reserves available to their roots.

Dense mats or mounds of closely knit stems and small leaves are common in dry landscapes. If the plants have larger leaves, which is sometimes the case if they are leathery or hairy, then they would normally form a rosette, rising centrally and then leaning out to clothe the ground around them. These shuttlecock shapes blend perfectly with rounded hummocks and flat carpets to create the common identity of the dry garden.

The effects of form and texture are sometimes thought to be more important than *colour* in gardens. Form and texture do last longer than flower displays, but the hues and tones of other plant parts are also visible, so colour cannot be ignored, even if it's not your thing. Colour shouldn't cause angst though – in the man-made world colours can clash, but it doesn't happen in nature because of the whole harmonious background blend that makes perfect sense of any temporary, random encounter between, say, orange and pink. Solid blocks of bedding plants with their unnaturally large flowers are probably the only serious colour offenders in gardens, so as with everything else, you should just have fun. Rainbow mixtures, colour themes and monochrome borders all have their place and help create the mood of the garden. Striking contrasts and subtle harmonies may happen by accident, but they're more fulfilling when they suddenly appear months after the original inspiration of putting two plants together. So it's worth thinking about colour and making the most of it.

Near the house, close to the water butts, is a good place for colourful seasonal plantings. Wherever you're especially looking for drought resistance, silver foliage is likely to feature strongly, so how that associates with other colours is worth a thought. Yellow flowers aren't the best companion for silver, but then, many silver leaved plants are in the daisy family and have exactly that. Picking the flowers off is one option, albeit slightly obsessive, but purple foliage combines well with these plants,

Enjoy colour: buddleja, ligustrum, hemerocallis and tamarisk, with the richer purples of berberis and cotinus.

giving strength and depth that remove the 'wishy-washyness' from silver and yellow. All colours, from hot zingy oranges to soft mauves and pinks, seem to complement purple foliage, as of course they do green foliage, so feel free and experiment. There is no set look to water-efficient gardens, and though dry gardens may prompt certain shapes, textures and background tones, flower colours are there to be played with.

Harmony and contrast
Harmony is where plants and materials are selected and combined for their common features so they blend together. They may be similar in form, texture or colour, with slight differences to provide subtle variation but there are no startling contrasts. When selecting plants for certain conditions, like very dry and exposed or wet and shady, their natural ability to grow in that environment will give them a certain type of appearance. Since they are all suited to the same conditions, the inherent ecological harmony will appear in the garden as a visual harmony.

Sharp contrasts in form, texture or colour create points of emphasis and stimulate the eye, as opposed to the more restful effect of harmonies. Too much contrast can make for a busy, fussy garden, where it might be hard to relax, but lack of contrast can be dull. When combining plants for contrasting effect, it often works best if they have at least something in common. A narrow upright plant and a rounded one, both with smallish green leaves, would appear as a fairly natural contrast. But if the leaves of one were large and yellow, and on the other they were feathery purple, the effect would be far more startling. If your garden was full of contrasts like that, you'd probably always be wanting to take a country walk.

The garden at one with itself

However you want your garden to be, the important thing for most of us is that it's fit for purpose and pleasing to the eye. The appearance is indeed often the main purpose, and although beauty is in the eye of the beholder, there are some universal principles which, when applied to design, can ensure that most other people like your garden as well.

Unity is the overriding principle of design, as discord makes us ill at ease. The need for the garden to be an integrated whole, of greater value than the sum of its parts, is probably the main benefit of designing the garden at all. A visual unity must be found with the house and the surrounds, as well as within the garden itself. All of your thoughts about style and character will be in the name of unity, and full regard to this essential oneness should continue throughout the design process.

By mimicking vegetation and other materials that occur within sight of the garden, you can create a feeling of mutual belonging between the garden and its surrounds. In the same way, repetition of plants and construction materials in your garden will help give it a single identity. Failure to achieve unity in a garden normally arises from an overwhelming desire to have plants, features or materials for their own sake rather than for their contribution to the garden. For the plantaholics amongst us, this doesn't mean that you should walk quickly past every garden centre or plant sale. Just that, unless you have some vision of how something will fit into the garden, it will probably only add to an increasing sense of muddle.

The dry garden, and its use of drought tolerant plants, is a case in point as regards unity. Fitting spiky leaved exotics and expanses of gravel into a lush setting of green lawns, rhododendrons and rhubarb could turn out to be a mistake. If it works, then that would be because they were visually partitioned from, or gently graded into, the greenness, in a way that made them belong. Unity is most conspicuous in its own absence, so if you imagine how something will look, and it seems right, then actually it will probably look right.

All the other principles of design serve to enhance unity and help us to do what we want and have fun with our gardens, without sacrificing that essential quality. Harmony and contrast can be developed through selecting plants and materials for their form, texture and colour, so contributing to other unifying qualities like proportion, scale, balance and rhythm. If you're not an arty person and feel uncomfortable with these terms, please be assured that they're just common sense. Any place you've seen that looks nice will have some or all of these qualities, so it's helpful to bear them in mind as you design your garden, choose your plants and decide how you want to place them.

Harmonious solidarity in their resistance to salt – elymus, erigeron and phormium down on the beach at Worthing.

CHAPTER 3

Plants

The plants recommended here represent a range of plants you can buy that should survive a few weeks in summer without rain or watering. They would need to be in a soil and position that suits them, and growing well with unrestricted, free range roots. This is only a selection of some of the plants that survive drought. There are many others, but these have been chosen to cover a range of requirements as shown in Chapter 5, along with other gardening information. Look there for plants with a particular purpose, for example plants for particular soils or conditions, plants for ground cover or hedging, plants for containers or borders.

Habitats and origins

The natural habitats of these plants, and the parts of the world they come from, are included to indicate the conditions they need in our gardens. How hardy they are against cold and frost is mentioned only when winter survival may be restricted primarily to gardens in the southern or western coastal parts of the UK, which applies especially to some of the species from different parts of the Southern Hemisphere, southwestern US and the Mediterranean region. Those described from other parts of Europe, across Asia and the eastern side of North America will generally be hardy throughout the UK.

The most common requirements of these plants are sunshine and free drainage. If heavy soils, winter wet and shade are amongst the conditions you are dealing with, look for plants from moist or woodland habitats. Really drought-resistant plants come from very dry places, which tend to be sunny because no plants grow big enough to cast much shade. But competition for water makes a woodland floor dry, and wet grassy streamsides can

Purple loosestrife, a species of marshes and river banks, is seen here naturalized in a dry rocky place by the sea.

become much drier in summer, so drought resistance is needed in a wide range of conditions. Plants are adapted to cope in so many ways that there are always some we can choose.

Height and spread

Soil and climate determine not only what grows where and whether it survives, but also how quickly it grows and how large it will get. The height and spread you can expect plants to reach is important to think about, but difficult to know for sure.

The imprecision of gardening can sometimes frustrate. How tall will it get? How wide will it spread? Well it depends on many things – the soil, the micro-climate, whether you prune it or the rabbits eat it, how long it stays there and how quickly it grows – but you do need some idea of size, albeit just a rough one. Many shrubs and trees will eventually get too big for the place you give them, but if it's only a bit too big, and the growth doesn't happen too quickly, pruning can normally contain it. Hard annual pruning may indeed be part of the plan when planting certain trees and large shrubs in small gardens – they change their identity to something much smaller. But generally with woody plants, they get just a bit bigger each year until they become small trees, large or medium shrubs and so on.

Non-woody plants reach their ultimate height far quicker than trees and shrubs, but growing conditions have a more palpable effect on how tall this actually is. Fertile soils, with high available moisture content, can produce ten or more times the annual growth you would get in the same species on poorer soils. It is the less fussy species, which grow in all sorts of soil, that are most likely to vary

The herb valerian, seen here as seed heads, reaches shoulder height in wet ground, but on dry soil stays tiny.

in this way. But all plants do to some extent, and watering or not, as the case may be, can produce the same variation. The heights suggested for the plants on the following pages are at the tall end of the range, reflecting good growing conditions, but poorer soils may well be preferred, producing smaller but sturdier and perhaps longer-lived plants.

Height and spread.

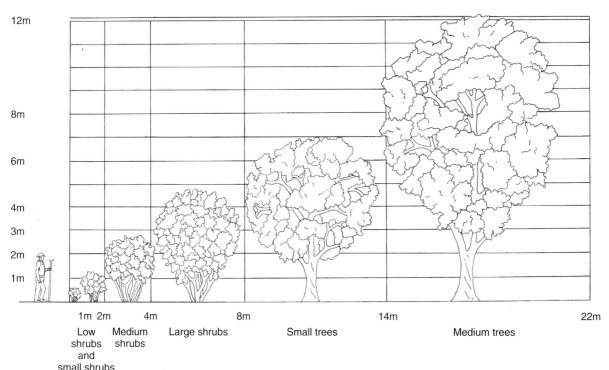

The sideways growth of many garden plants is contained by the proximity of walls, fences, neighbouring plants and the need for pruning them clear of paths and lawns. Some idea of how quickly, and how wide, they would spread if unrestricted, enables us to space them out sensibly and indeed, to buy the right amount of plants in the first place. Again, not being a precise science, guidelines are helpful. For many plants, the space they need equates roughly to their height, but we might give them a bit less with the intention of pruning gently or just allowing them to merge with neighbouring plants. The approximate height and space required for the different size categories of trees and shrubs is indicated here with each plant.

For plants that you know are particularly broad spreading or upright, you would give more or less space accordingly. Also, if you are planting a group of the same species so they grow together as one, as is nearly always the case with non-woody plants, less space would be given to each individual (*see* 'Detailed Design of a Bed or Border' on page 25).

Some idea of their ultimate size is essential though, particularly with the larger woody plants described here. These trees, shrubs and climbers form the permanent framework of our gardens and are best left where they are planted if at all possible. But in the right place, with enough space to grow, they are long lived, with strong roots, and are self-sufficient for water except under the most extreme circumstances. It's a rare thing that mature trees and shrubs need watering to survive, so the ones described here are just some that you can expect to succeed in a severely dry summer, perhaps in conjunction with shade or winter waterlogging.

What's in a name?

When referring to plants, we use species, and sometimes, cultivar names. Species occur naturally and are named using two words. The first word is the genus that the species belongs to, and the second is the species itself.

Each entry shown alphabetically on the following pages is a genus, such as Abelia, Abutilon or Acacia. The two species described in the genus Acacia are *Acacia dealbata* and *Acacia pravissima*.

Just because a genus is included here does not

The cultivar Coreopsis verticillata *'Zagreb' is thought to be more drought-resistant than other cultivars of that species.*

mean that all species in that genus are drought resistant. Any plant belonging to one of the species shown, however, should be fairly drought resistant, even if it is some sort of variant from within that species. These variants are normally cultivated varieties, or cultivars, so called because they do not occur naturally. They have been especially selected for gardening because of their leaf colour, flower size, neat shape, or some other attribute, possibly their extra drought resistance.

The cultivar name comes after the species name and so appears, for example, as *Acer platanoides* 'Crimson king', a purple leaved variant of the species we commonly call Norway maple.

On rare occasions the variant may be naturally occurring and referred to officially as either a subspecies, a variety or a form, e.g. *Coronolla valentina* subsp. *glauca*. The terms 'variety' and 'form', though, are often used by gardeners informally to mean any kind of variant, including a cultivar. Such casual use of the terms is made here.

Most of the species and cultivars mentioned here should be fairly easy to obtain from nurseries or seed suppliers, which you can source by using the RHS's Plant Finder book or online facility. Many of the plants recommended here hold the RHS Award of Garden Merit.

Tamarisks are normally shrubs, but this one in Worthing is trained and maintained as a small standard tree.

WOODY PLANTS

Trees

Species that normally grow with a single trunk, and reach up to about the height of a bungalow, are trees. They are often used as focal points in gardens, taking pride of place, so need to be chosen carefully. Find one that brings as much delight, for as much of the year as possible. Once in the ground, and growing happily, it will need very little attention, but a fair bit of watering may be needed in order to get to that stage. How much, and for how long, will depend largely on the size of the nursery plant that you buy (*see* page 26).

Shrubs

Shrubs are smaller than trees and they do not have a single trunk. They may be planted en masse, as ground cover or hedging, in little groups or as specimens. Whether they are evergreen or deciduous has a big impact on the garden, as does their stature, above eye level or not. They are major contributors of winter display, through flowers, berries, and coloured foliage, and many are in full bloom at the time when the garden awakes in spring. Apart from the watering and weeding to get them started, and with some, the pruning thereafter, they take care of themselves.

Climbers and wall shrubs

Climbers are naturally adapted to climb over things. They twine around branches and wires or have special adaptations that stick them to surfaces. Wall shrubs are planted against walls for protection or because they look tidier that way. Between them these plants help ensure that you have got something growing in every place you possibly can – over a shed, up a wall, through a tree. This, in turn, ensures maximum value for rainfall.

Abelia (small shrub, medium shrub)
Normally seen as the garden hybrid *A.* × *grandi-flora*, these are easy plants to grow, in a wide range of soils. Their elegant arching branches bear shiny leaves, evergreen through warmer winters, and lots of small, slightly pinkish white flowers from mid-summer to autumn. Then, after the petals have gone, bronze-red autumnal tints are seen in the persistent flower sepals and any leaves which are preparing to fall. *A.* × *grandiflora* is a medium sized shrub, but various smaller cultivars are also available. *A.* × *g.* 'Confetti' has variegated foliage while on *A.* 'Edward Goucher' the new leaves are bronze and the flowers lilac-pink.

Abutilon megapotamicum.

Abutilon (medium shrub, large shrub)
These are mainly shrubs from forests and rocky places in South America, and although not very frost hardy, can be excellent deciduous flowering shrubs for sunny walls. *A. megapotamicum* is one of the smaller species, with really distinctive flowers of red and yellow that hang from its branches through late summer. *A. vitifolium* is larger with grey felted leaves and mauve flowers earlier in the season.

Acacia dealbata.

Acacia (small tree)
Mainly from seasonally dry tropical regions, it is the ones from Tasmania and the cooler parts of Australia that can be grown in gardens such as those of southern England. *A. dealbata*, the silver wattle, is one of the hardiest. With feathery, evergreen leaves of a silvery green colour, it earns its keep all year round. Then in winter, masses of scented, fluffy spherical flowers light up the tree for weeks until spring. The further north you are, the greater the risk with frost, but south facing walls can provide useful protection. *A. pravissima* is smaller – similar in flower but with leaves reduced to flattened stalks.

Acca (medium shrub)
A. sellowiana, the pineapple guava, comes from dry shrubby slopes in South America. It is generally happy outside in southern England but will need the protection of a sunny wall in colder areas. With grey-green leaves, white felted beneath, it is grown

for the extraordinary flowers that appear in summer – rich red fleshy edible petals with white margins, and tufts of red stamens have a truly exotic appeal. Most of the cultivars are selected for their edible fruits, but you need a really warm garden for a worthwhile crop. It is normally sold simply as *A. sellowiana*, or sometimes in the form *A. s.* 'Variegata', which is well worth looking for.

Acer (small tree, medium tree)
These are the maples, deciduous trees which occur in various habitats across North America, Europe and Asia. Popular in gardens for elegance, and beauty of foliage, it has to be said that it is the least drought tolerant Japanese species that best display these qualities. For tougher maples, more tolerant of dryness and exposure, there are coloured leaved forms of the Norway maple, *A. platanoides*, and the American box elder, *A. negundo*. *A. p.* 'Crimson King' is medium sized with deep purple foliage and intriguing red-tinged yellow flowers in spring. *A. n.* 'Flamingo' is a small tree with very pretty white variegated leaves that start off pink and green. The European field maple, *Acer campestre*, with soft yellow autumn tints, is equally easy to please. *A. c.* 'Elsrijk' is one with a dense upright crown, ideal for small gardens.

Ailanthus (medium shrub, large tree)
A. altissima, of Chinese woodlands, is called the tree of heaven because that's where its strong and rapid growth will soon reach. It can be grown as a shrub though, by cutting it hard back to the ground every year or two. The resulting shoots, with massive divided leaves, will emerge like a giant fern to way over head height. Left alone to become a tree, it is no less attractive, with a soft grey, slightly stripy trunk, and broad open crown laden with large tropical looking leaves through the growing season.

Albizia (small tree)
A. julibrissin is the silk tree, from open woodland right across Asia. It is a beautiful small deciduous tree with a dome shaped crown, fine feathery foliage, and fluffy pinkish white flowers through summer. It definitely has the exotic look, but is surprisingly hardy, in all but the frostiest places.

Albizia julibrissin.

Alnus (medium tree)
Though perhaps normally thought of as large forest trees for very wet places, there is one alder, *A. cordata* from southern Italy, that also copes well with dry and exposed conditions. And for such an unfussy plant, it has a remarkably noble appearance. Medium sized and slender in shape, with bold, really glossy, heart-shaped leaves, its bare winter stems are attractively adorned with catkins and cone-like fruits. Growth can be quick and excessive, but in dry soil, without irrigation, that is unlikely to be a problem. It is one, however, that you should keep well away from buildings if your soil is clay.

Aralia (large shrub)
A. elata is the Japanese angelica tree, although it is actually more of a large woodland shrub, grown for the enormous sprays of white flowers it produces in late summer and, more importantly, for the tropical appearance of its large divided leaves. On falling in autumn the leaves expose the sparsely arranged stout prickly stems that stand with an intriguing skeletal appearance in the winter garden. Variegated forms are well worth having but expensive to buy. It's a shame their suckers come up green.

Aralia elata *'Variegata'*.

Arbutus unedo.

Arbutus (small tree)
A. unedo is the Killarney strawberry tree from rocky woods and hillsides in southern Ireland and the Mediterranean region. It's a small spreading tree with glossy evergreen leaves and clusters of little white flowers that appear, in autumn, alongside the fruits from the previous year's flowering. They are edible and sort of strawberry-like in looks, but don't compare in culinary terms. *A.* × *andrachnoides* is a related hybrid with beautiful cinnamon-red bark.

Artemisia (small shrub)

Artemisia *'Powis Castle'*.

This is a large genus of small aromatic shrubs and perennials (*see* page 87), from dry slopes, cliff tops and other arid habitats. Mostly grown for their grey-green or silver, finely divided foliage, the small yellowish late summer flowers do little to enhance their appearance. *A.* 'Powis Castle', of European parentage, exemplifies the decorative qualities of the genus; it's a small evergreen shrub that forms a soft billowing mass of fine lacy, silvery leaves. One of the parents, *A. absinthium*, or wormwood, is often grown as the cultivar 'Lambrook Silver' which has similar qualities. Lad's Love, *A. abrotanum*, is slightly taller, more upright and greener, with sweetly scented foliage.

Aucuba (medium shrub)

A. japonica, the spotted laurel, is normally seen with its large leathery evergreen leaves splashed yellow, but the wild plant, of Asian forests, is plain green. It is one of those species with separate male and female plants. Only the latter can produce the clusters of bright red fruits, but a male plant must be around to pollinate. *A. j.* 'Crotonifolia' is a good choice for heavily spotted leaves. Though normally female, some nurseries sell a male companion under the same name. For large red fruits amongst dark green leaves on a neat compact plant, try *A. j.* 'Rozannie'.

Berberis (small, medium shrub)

The barberries are mainly from rocky upland areas around the Northern Hemisphere and in South America. Evergreen or deciduous, in a range of sizes, the one thing in common is their prickliness. But if that's not what you're looking for, don't be put off. They are great givers of colour, from spring flowers fruit or foliage, and ask for little in return. *B.* × *stenophylla* has gracefully arching branches with yellow flowers, and *B. darwinii* gives a profuse display of rich orange flowers. They are both South American evergreens of medium size. From Japan is the deciduous medium sized *B. thunbergii* with yellow flowers, red berries, stunning autumn foliage, and available in various coloured leaved forms (*see* page 63). *B. wilsoniae* is a small mounded deciduous Chinese shrub with great bunches of coral pink berries, and if it's prickles you do want, try the evergreen *B. julianae*.

Berberis darwinii.

Betula (medium tree)

These are the birches, from cold northerly regions around the globe. They are beautifully poised trees, sparsely branched with slender stems, golden autumn leaves and wonderful bark. The common European silver birch, *Betula pendula*, and the North American paper birch, *B. papyrifera*, have all these attributes. Multi-stemmed specimens available from nurseries are well worth seeking.

Brachyglottis (small shrub, medium shrub)

These evergreen shrubs from rocky New Zealand coasts have grey or green leaves, white on the underside, and yellow daisy flowers in summer. *B.* 'Sunshine' is particularly hardy and free flowering, forming a dense low mound. Useful for sheltering coastal sites is the taller *B. rotundifolia*, and *B. repanda* is something far more exotic. Suitable only for warmer gardens, it is really big and bold in leaf and flower.

Buddleja alternifola.

Buddleja globosa.

Buddleja (medium shrub, large shrub, small tree)

This is a large group of shrubs from dry stony habitats. Most famous is *Buddleja davidii*, the butterfly bush, which is commonly naturalized in Europe on waste ground and buildings. Medium sized and deciduous, it produces large heads of fragrant flowers, on long arching stems, in late summer. Cultivars are selected particularly for the length and colour of their flower heads. *B. d.* 'Black Knight', 'Royal Red' and 'White Profusion' are notable. *B.* 'Pink Delight' and *B.* 'Lochinch' are similar hybrids, the latter with distinct grey felted young leaves and heads of violet-blue, orange centred flowers. All these are of Chinese descent, as is the extraordinary *B. alternifolia*, often appearing as a small weeping tree, its long pendulous branches wreathed with fragrant lilac flowers in June. Quite different again, and from South America, is *B. globosa*, with its stiffer, more upright habit and spherical heads of orange flowers in June.

Butia (small tree)

B. capitata, the jelly palm, from South America, is the hardiest of the palms that have feather, as opposed to fan-shaped leaves. Evergreen and extremely long, atop a short stout trunk, they rise and arch elegantly, creating the classic, tropical palm look. Large sprays of yellow flowers, followed by sweet jelly-like fruits, add interest in summer. It is hardy enough for most gardens in southern England, and if you're thinking of trying it, look out for another feather-leaved species, the date palm relative, *Phoenix canariensis*.

Buxus (small shrub, medium shrub, large shrub)
B. sempervirens is the common box, grown for centuries in Europe as a hedging plant and topiary subject. The wild species, a large shrub, occurs throughout Europe and beyond, in dry woodlands, typically on chalky soils. It's the solid greenness we grow it for, which can be moulded into anything through pruning and trimming. Left alone, the fragrant yellow spring flowers are loved by bees, so it's OK to have a box that isn't a ball or a bunny rabbit. Variations on the common box are selected for their vigour and leaf colour. 'Handsworthensis' makes a good tall hedge while the blue-green leaved 'Blauer Heinz' and variegated 'Elegantissima' are more compact. *B. microphylla* is smaller and, as the cultivar 'Faulkner', is useful for dwarf hedging as it seems less prone than others to box blight (*see* page 146).

Callistemon (medium shrub)
These are the Australian bottlebrushes, which, in the wild, occur in a range of different conditions, sometimes actually quite wet and boggy. Their leathery evergreen leaves give the impression of drought resistance though, and once established, they generally are. Hardiness can be a problem, but *C. citrinus* is usually all right, surviving in reasonably protected gardens, even in northern England. Often grown as the cultivar 'Splendens', it is an elegant medium sized shrub with a long summer display of bright red bottlebrush flowers on gracefully arching branches.

Calocedrus (large tree)
C. decurrens, known as the incense cedar, is a conifer from the drier spots of the forests of north-west America. It is one if the best trees you'll find if looking for something tall and narrow. The perfect column formed by its trunk and branches is clothed to the ground with vertical sprays of shiny dark evergreen foliage, giving it a subtle richness of texture and colour. This species may be sold as *C. d.* 'Columnaris' or as *Libocedrus decurrens*, but check the description of the tree you're buying to ensure that it is an upright growing form.

Caragana (medium shrub, small tree)
C. arborescens is the pea tree of riversides and rocky slopes in northern China and Siberia. Generally only available as cultivars, this small deciduous tree with yellow spring flowers is most noted for its incredible resilience to cold, exposure and poor infertile soils. *C. a.* 'Lorbergii' has graceful arching branches, and foliage in which the small leaflets of the species are reduced to slender 'blades of grass'. *C. a.* 'Pendula' is a dramatically weeping form, and in *C. a.* 'Walker' the fine texture and pendulous shape are combined.

Caryopteris (small shrub)
This is nearly always grown as the hybrid species, *C. × clandonensis*. Its parents are small deciduous shrubs of dry rocky places in the Far East, but the displays of blue flowers during late summer/autumn are much improved in hybrid cultivars such as *C. × c.* 'Heavenly Blue' and the darker 'Kew Blue'. They are mound forming shrubs, with grey-green leaves, and flowers that occur in clusters along the young stems.

Ceanothus (small shrub, medium shrub)
These evergreen and deciduous shrubs, known as Californian lilacs, originate mainly on the dry slopes of western North America. Their bobbleheads of tiny flowers appear either in late spring or mid summer, often completely saturating the plant in some shade of blue. The early cultivars are all evergreen. 'Blue Mound' is fairly low and spreading, while 'Dark Star' is medium sized with

Ceanothus *'Dark Star'*.

ABOVE: Ceanothus *'Gloire de Versailles'*.

RIGHT: Ceanothus *'Marie Simon'*.

arching branches. Included amongst the later cultivars are some deciduous shrubs of small-medium size such as 'Gloires de versailles' and the pink 'Marie Simon'.

Ceratostigma (small shrub)

C. willmottianum is a small deciduous shrub from dry stony slopes in China. It has striking, rich blue flowers, which occur from late summer to coincide with the red tinted autumn foliage. *C. griffithii* is similar but has leaves that often persist through winter and *C. plumbaginoides*, an herbaceous species, stays lower at about knee height.

Ceratostigma wilmottianum.

Cercis (small tree)

C. siliquastrum is the Judas tree from stony slopes in the Mediterranean region and eastwards. Small but spreading, it is grown for the distinctive blue-green heart shaped leaves and profuse spring display of bright rosy pink flowers that sprout all along the bare stems, right back into the thickest branches. It is a relative of peas, and the flowers have a refreshing mange tout-like taste, but you'll never eat them all, so most will turn to attractive purple pods before the soft yellow hews of leaf fall. *C. canadensis*, the North American redbud, is popular in the coloured-leaved form *C. c.* 'Forest Pansy', but it doesn't flower nearly so well.

Choisya (medium shrub)

C. ternata, the Mexican orange blossom, is an evergreen shrub of rocky slopes. It has a neat rounded shape and clusters of white scented flowers that show up perfectly against the shiny dark green aromatic leaves in late spring, and again later in summer. *C. t.* 'Sundance' has bright yellow foliage but is not attractive in flower. *C.* 'Aztec Pearl' has beautifully fine textured dark green leaves.

Cercis canadensis *'Forest Pansy'*.

Choisya ternata *'Aztec Pearl'*.

Cistus *'Silver Pink'*.

Cistus × dansereaui *'Decumbens'*.

Halimium lasianthum.

Cistus (small shrub)

These are the sun roses from hot dry rocky hills around the Mediterranean. They are evergreen shrubs, often with aromatic foliage and showy 'rose-like' flowers. Cold wet winters in heavy soils can cause them problems, and they are quite short-lived anyway so may need replacing after just a few years. The individual flowers don't last long either, but there are loads of them which keep coming for several weeks from early summer. Most of the showiest sun roses are low growing cultivars of hybrid species, and there are many to choose from. *C.* × *pulverulentus* 'Sunset' has silvery-green leaves and rich magenta flowers. Similar, but with softer flower colour, is *C.* 'Silver Pink', and *C.* × *dansereaui*, with green sticky leaves, is one of a number that have petals distinctively marked at their base. Yellow petals don't occur in Cistus, but they are found amongst the closely related genus *Halimium*.

Colutea (tall shrub)

C. arborescens, the bladder senna, is a tall deciduous shrub of dry Mediterranean slopes. Its clusters
of yellow pea flowers appear for weeks throughout
summer amongst the pale green leaves, and are followed in autumn by large inflated translucent seed
pods. *C. × media* 'Copper Beauty' has bright orange
flowers and pink tinted seed pods.

Convolvulus (small shrub)

Convolvulus cneorum.

C. cneorum, from cliffs by the Mediterranean,
must be embarrassed by the behaviour of its close
cousin, the bindweed. Infinitely more refined, this
small rounded shrub, with silky smooth, silvery
leaves, shows its family connection through white,
funnel-shaped flowers of the kind that appear, so
unwanted, in our shrubs and hedges. But in this
delicate little shrub, they open from pink buds in
early summer, and harmonize well with the foliage,
bringing no such grief to gardeners.

Cordyline australis.

Cordyline (small tree)

C. australis is the cabbage palm from New Zealand. It's not actually a palm, but it has that look
about it, and it is hardy in most parts of the UK.
Young plants chosen for their long evergreen
sword-shaped leaves will eventually form a sparsely
branched trunk bearing tufts of foliage and, in early
summer, enormous sprays of creamy white flowers.
There are various coloured leaved forms, but they
are generally slower growing, and not as hardy, so
less likely to make a tree.

Coronilla (small shrub)

C. valentina subsp. *glauca*, the Mediterranean
crownvetch, is a small evergreen shrub of dry rocky
slopes. It is grown in gardens for the clusters of
fragrant yellow flowers that appear mainly during
winter and spring. The soft blue-green foliage is
finely divided and delicate looking, with creamy-
white margins in the cultivar 'Variegata'.

Coronilla valentina *subsp*. glauca.

Cotoneaster *'Rothschildianus'*.

Cotoneaster (small, medium, large shrub)
This is a large genus of shrubs native to open, or wooded, dry rocky places mainly in China and the Himalayas. Deciduous or evergreen, they include creeping ground coverers and small trees. All have tiny flowers, usually white and in clusters, followed by colourful fruits in autumn, and many are elegant of form, with beautiful arching branches. Their common use in municipal landscapes, sometimes leading gardeners to shun them, only goes to reflect these qualities and the fact that they demand so little. *C. conspicuus* 'Decorus' forms a dense low mound of tiny evergreen leaves and gives a prolific display of red fruits. *C. horizontalis*, with its distinctive herringbone branching pattern, is deciduous and makes a good wall shrub and groundcover too. The archetypal ground cover though is *C. dammeri*, evergreen, vigorous in growth and flat to the ground. Two of medium size are *C. franchetii*, with gracefully spreading branches, and the more upright *C. simonsii*, which is good for hedging. They are evergreen to varying degrees, with bright orange-red fruits. *C.* 'Rothschildianus' is taller still, an elegantly formed evergreen with long-lasting yellow fruits.

Cotoneaster horizontalis.

Crataegus (small tree)

C. monogyna (hawthorn) is famous in England as the mainstay of rural hedgerows, but it belongs to a worldwide tribe of small rounded, usually thorny trees, which are excellent for home gardens. The American species are the most garden worthy, with their flowers, fruit, autumn leaf colour and beautiful spreading crowns. *C. persimilis* 'Prunifolia', the broadleaved cockspur thorn, has it all. In early summer, its rounded crown, spangled with heads of pink and white flowers, recalls the sweet natured, happy trees of children's story books. Then when the fruits appear, and the shiny green leaves get set to fall, it seems there are all the colours of autumn on one tree. Other Americans of a similar ilk are *C. crus-galli* and *C.* × *lavallei*, but then hawthorn itself, when not a hedge, is a beautiful tree in full May flower. For really striking, dark pink flowers, there is a cultivar of the midland hawthorn called *C. laevigata* 'Paul's Scarlet'.

Cupressus (medium tree)

C. sempervirens is the Mediterranean cypress, the really slender upright one that we associate with Italian landscapes. A medium sized evergreen with dense sprays of dark or sometimes slightly greyish foliage, it is planted for the clean vertical accent it gives. This is sometimes spoilt though, if the branches pull away under the weight of the cones, making its silhouette ragged. The cultivars 'Pyramidalis' and 'Green Pencil' are selected for their particularly narrow shape. *C. arizonica* var. *glabra*, from north-west America, is fairly narrow in shape with blue-green leaves, or a vivid steely blue in the cultivar 'Blue Ice'.

Cytisus × praecox *'Albus'*.

Cytisus (small shrub, large shrub)

These are the brooms, or at least some of them (*see* page 56), from dry open hills and mountain heaths, mainly in the Mediterranean region. Most are deciduous with tiny leaves, or no leaves at all, on the dense mass of wiry stems that have a lively greenness even in winter. It's the flowers they're grown for though: typically small, pea-like,

Cupressus sempervirens.

Cytisus battandieri.

yellowish and borne in spring or early summer along the stems, so as to accentuate the broom's natural arching habit. Both the plants themselves and their flower displays are short-lived, though spectacular in their glory moments. The common species, *C. scoparius*, of sandy heaths in the UK is a good plant itself, but we normally grow the various hybrids and cultivars. *C. × kewensis* is a very low ground cover with creamy coloured flowers. Taller but still very compact are *C. × praecox* 'Allgold' and *C. × p.* 'Albus'. *C.* 'Lena' is one of several cultivars with strong reds in its flowers. Growing much taller and almost tree-like is *Cytisus battandieri*, the pineapple broom from Morocco. It has much larger, silvery leaves and dense clusters of sweetly fragrant yellow flowers in mid summer.

Danae (small shrub)

D. racemosa, the Alexandrian laurel, is a small evergreen of the woodland floor, in mountainous regions of Turkey and Iran. It forms a dense clump of arching shoots that bear really shiny green, leaf-like stems (*see* page 16), which perfectly complement the red berries that appear after hot summers. *Ruscus aculeatus*, the butcher's broom, is a close relative growing in woodlands through much of Europe and beyond. While it is stiffer, tougher, and prickly, lacking the elegance of *Danae*, it has a tolerance of dry shade that's pretty much second to none.

Erica arborea *var.* alpina.

Elaeagnus (large shrub)

These are large deciduous or evergreen shrubs from poor dry soils in exposed locations around the Northern Hemisphere. Grown mostly for foliage colour, but also for flower scent and berries, a key attribute for gardeners is their toughness in the face of cold and salt laden winds. *E. × ebbingei* is an evergreen of Japanese descent with sweetly scented, though inconspicuous, autumn flowers. Variegated forms such as 'Gilt Edge' make good foliage plants. Among the deciduous varieties *E. commutata*, the silver berry from America, is a thicket forming shrub with really silvery leaves and fruits which has fragrant flowers in May. But the best for scent are *E. angustifolia*, the Russian olive with edible fruits, and from the Far East the ornamentally fruiting *E. umbellata*, with their soft parts covered with the silver-scaly sheen that characterizes the genus, giving the impression of having been decorated with some kind of paint spray. This quality is also seen in the closely related sea buckthorn, *Hippophae rhamnoides*, a large European shrub of sea cliffs and sand dunes, which on female plants produces attractive orange berries.

Erica (small shrub, medium shrub)
Heaths and heathers certainly look drought-resistant. Their tiny moisture conserving leaves and low spreading growth are just what is needed on windy moors. But those places are often quite wet, and the roots are not the type that go looking for water. The summer flowering bell heather (*E. cinerea*) and ling (*Calluna vulgaris*) are species of the drier heathlands, with fairly low water demand, but it's the much taller Mediterranean tree heath, *E. arborea*, which can really put up with hot and dry. It remains medium sized in the particularly hardy *E. a.* var. *alpina*, and has long pyramidal clusters of honey scented white flowers in spring. Most commonly seen in gardens, and less demanding than most of acid soil, is the winter flowering *E. carnea*, a low shrub of conifer woods and stony slopes. Its different cultivars give a flower colour range from white through all sorts of pink to deep reds, and there's lots of choice in foliage colour too.

Eriobotrya (small tree)
E. japonica is the loquat, a small spreading tree from woodlands in China and Japan. The tropical look of its big shiny leaves (*see* page 33) is enough reason to grow it, so white fragrant autumn flowers and juicy spring fruits would be a real bonus.

Escallonia (medium shrub)

These South American shrubs of open hillsides and cliffs are grown in gardens for their summer flowers and glossy evergreen foliage. *E.* 'Donard Radiance' captures the full spirit, with flowers of a beautiful soft rose-red and shiny, deep green leaves. For paler flowers, of pink with white, 'Apple Blossom' is a good choice. While both flower fairly early in summer, there are others such as *E.* 'Iveyi', with large heads of white flowers, and *E. rubra*, that are later. Splendid form from gracefully arching branches can also been found in the genus – look for either *E.* 'Edinensis' or 'Langleyensis'.

Eucalyptus (medium shrub, small tree, medium tree)
It's not surprising to find good drought resistant species amongst the gum trees of Australia. They have adapted to almost all soils and climates that occur there, and, with their sparse bony branches, shedding bark and blue-grey waxy leaves, they certainly appear in harmony with arid environments. The key issues for gardeners when choosing are whether they are small enough and hardy enough. The snow gum, *E. pauciflora* subsp. *niphophila*, ticks both boxes well, and normally branches low to produce multiple stems with beautiful cream and grey patchwork bark and narrow lance shaped leaves. The hardiest is probably *E. gunnii* (*see* page 34), but it grows far too large for most gardens. When young and small however, its grey-green foliage gives a soft airy effect that can be retained in shrub form by pruning hard back, close to the ground, every year or two.

Euonymus (small shrub, medium shrub, large shrub)
E. europaeus is the wild spindle tree of woods and hedgerows. Other species are mainly from the Far East, and include some very popular evergreen shrubs. The spindle itself forms a large spreading shrub, catching the eye in autumn when the rose-pink fruits, amongst reddening leaves, split to reveal bright orange seeds. *E. e.* 'Red Cascade' is especially selected for its autumn display, while *E. alatus* is a medium sized deciduous shrub from China/Japan, with astounding autumn leaf colour.

Escallonia *'Iveyi'*.

Euonymus europaeus.

The evergreens are normally selected for their variegated foliage. The *E. fortunei* cultivars 'Emerald Gaiety', with white leaf margins, and 'Emerald 'n' Gold', are commonly planted for ground cover, while 'Silver Queen' is medium sized with striking white variegation and a fondness for climbing if given a wall. *E. japonicus* 'Microphyllus', a dense compact evergreen, is a good choice for a dwarf hedge.

Fabiana (medium shrub)

F. imbricata is a medium sized evergreen shrub from rocky slopes in the Andes. Its branches, clothed with tiny overlapping leaves, are plumes of green that turn white when the little tubular flowers open all over them in June. Not happy in the coldest winters, it is normally grown in the mauve flowered form, *violacea*, which seems a bit hardier.

Fabiana imbricata f. violacea.

Fraxinus (medium tree)

Although most ashes are rather large, there is one medium sized tree that is ideal for gardens. *F. ornus*, the manna ash, from woods and rocky places in southern Europe, forms a dense rounded crown, with large fluffy heads of creamy-white flowers in

Fraxinus ornus.

late spring, and deep reddish autumn leaf colour. An excellent specimen for lawns or sunny courtyards, it has a real Mediterranean feel to it. The slow growing, compact *F. o.* 'Meczek' is especially suited to small spaces, and *F. o.* 'Louisa Lady' has really rich autumn leaf colour. Another Mediterranean is *F. angustifolia*, which does get rather large, but the cultivar 'Raywood' is more compact, with no flowers to speak of, but a rounded head of finely textured foliage that turns to a luscious red grape colour before falling in autumn.

Fremontodendron californicum.

Fremontodendron (large shrub)

F. californicum is a large vigorous evergreen that forms thickets on dry rocky slopes. Suited best to warm sheltered gardens, it produces yellow saucer shaped flowers from spring through to autumn. A particularly flowery cultivar is *F.* 'California Glory'.

Garrya (large shrub)

G. elliptica, the silk-tassel bush, is an evergreen from dry hills in the California region. Its catkins extend during late winter into long tassels of a pale silvery yellow that hang graciously from the branches for weeks. Mostly grown in the male form *G. e.* 'James Roof', it is an excellent plant for training against shady walls.

Genista (small shrub, large shrub)

These are more brooms (*see* page 52) originating in various dry habitats in Europe, the Mediterranean region and western Asia. All with yellow flowers, their foliage is usually very minimal and their shoots green. *G. Lydia* makes a low mound of slender arching stems which become covered in yellow in early summer. Flowering at the same time, and of similar shape but prickly, is *G. hispanica* or Spanish gorse. *G. tinctoria*, the dyer's greenwood, is small and upright, bearing vertical heads of flowers through summer. A much larger species is the slightly less hardy Mount Etna broom, *G. aetnensis*. Its elegant leafless stems cast almost no shade and produce bare fragrant flowers in July and August. *Spartium junceum*, the Spanish broom, is a medium sized shrub from dry rocky places. It has bright green, but almost leafless cylindrical stems and large heads of fragrant, golden yellow pea flowers for weeks through summer.

Genista Lydia.

Genista aetnensis.

Ginkgo (large tree)

G. biloba is the remarkable maidenhair tree, which has somehow survived unchanged since the days 200 million years ago when it grew throughout the world. So primitive, compared with our other trees, yet it has such a lot to offer modern gardeners, growing tall, but only slowly, and staying upright and narrow until old age. The curious fan-shaped leaves turn a soft yellow before falling in autumn, and its legendry survival bears testament to the tough unfussiness and independence that it shows in gardens. There are named cultivars, with particularly upright form, and some are male, which may be preferred due to the unpleasant smell of the fruits that will eventually occur on female trees.

Gleditsia (medium tree)

G. triacanthos is the honey locust from dry stony hills in North America. The species itself is a large elegant tree, with finely divided leaves and, after a warm summer, long shiny brown seed pods. Really too large for most home gardens, it is normally grown as *G. t.* 'Sunburst', which glows with the bright yellow of its young leaves. The canopy is not dense, and with a long season of leaflessness it is a good tree for growing above shrubs and perennials.

Gleditsia triacanthos *'Sunburst'*.

Grevillea (medium shrub)

Grevillea rosmarinifolia.

G. rosmarinifolia is a stiffly branched Australian shrub with tiny evergreen leaves. It normally grows up to about eye level, producing spidery, crimson flowers that show off well against the deep green foliage. Though not the hardiest plant in the South of England, it not only survives the coldest months but blooms through them, continuing on until early summer. *G.* 'Canberra Gem' is more vigorous, with bright pinkish-red flowers.

Griselinia (large shrub)
G. littoralis is a tall evergreen from New Zealand, where its natural adaptation to harsh coastal conditions makes it frequently used in seaside gardens elsewhere. There are no flowers or fruits to speak of – only leaves which, close to, have a strange not quite real, artificial feel. They are coloured a fresh, lively green though, without the sombreness that other evergreens may bestow on the winter garden.

Gymnocladus (medium tree)
G. dioica is the Kentucky coffee tree, from fairly deep rich soils in that part of the world. It can grow quite tall, but only very slowly, so the smallish stature normally seen serves to emphasize the size and elegance of its leaves. Up to one meter long by half a meter wide, and much divided, they unfurl with a pink tinge and fall a clear yellow. It is for these that the tree is planted, and not for its flowers, which are shy in appearing and modest when they do.

Hebe (small shrub, medium shrub)
These evergreen shrubs, mainly from rocky mountainsides and woods in New Zealand, are grown for leaf colour, texture, their neat, often rounded shape, and spectacular, long-lasting flower displays. Of course not every hebe can boast all of these, but many get close. It's the whipcord hebes, with tiny scale-like leaves and those with very small, waxy leaves, that are the hardiest and the most drought tolerant. Though less bright and flowery than the larger leaved types, they are grown mainly for foliage effect and their compact neat shape. *H. ochracea* 'James Stirling' is a whipcord type with arching branches bearing conifer-like foliage in a strange

Hebe rakaiensis.

Hebe *'Great Orme'*.

ochre-yellow colour, and has small spikes of white flowers in early summer. So too does *H. rakaiensis*, a small leaved type, which though more prominent in flower, is grown largely for its really tidy, knee-high hummocks of glossy green foliage. With slightly larger leaves, and a long-lasting display of purple blue flowers, *H. × franciscana* 'Blue Gem' is one of the best hebes for coastal locations. Another is the medium sized *H. salicifolia* with white flowers in long slender heads, characteristic of the various larger leaved garden hybrids such as 'Great Orme' and the lavender coloured 'Midsummer Beauty'. Small shrubs, and fairly hardy, they seem to flower forever.

Hedera (small shrub, climber)
H. helix is the common European ivy that climbs trees and covers the woodland floor. From dark glossy lobed leaves, it eventually produces stems with larger leaves of simpler shape that bear round heads of whitish flowers and black berries. Though an excellent wildlife plant it is normally grown in gardens for variegated foliage in cultivars such as 'Buttercup' and 'Glacier'. *H. h.* 'Erecta' is a small free-standing shrub with stiff upright branches. *H. hibernica*, the Irish ivy, with large shiny leaves, is a particularly effective ground cover.

Hypericum × inodorum *'Elstead'*.

Hypericum (small shrub, medium shrub)
The St John's worts that we grow in gardens are largely from woodland and mountain habitats in China. They may be evergreen or deciduous to varying degrees, but all have the characteristic yellow flowers, which appear in summer, often extended into autumn, and in some species are followed by attractive berries. *H. calycinum*, the Rose of Sharon, is a thuggish spreading ground cover, for use over large areas where it can't pick on other plants. Much better behaved is *H.* 'Hidcote', a rounded evergreen to chest height, with a long show of large golden yellow flowers. *H. androsaemum*, the European tutsan, has only very small flowers, but it is a good wildlife plant, with red berries that ripen to black. For the best berry display though, occurring in tandem with flowers, try *H. × inodorum* or one of its cultivars. There are also some smaller alpine hypericums such as *H. olympicum* 'Citrinum', with star-shaped lemon yellow flowers.

Ilex (small shrub, medium shrub, large shrub, small tree)

Ilex aquifolium, the common English holly, is native to much of Europe, North Africa and West Asia. Occurring in woodlands, it can itself reach the canopy, but is more often a small, fairly upright, evergreen understorey tree. Though sometimes accused of gloominess, its dark shiny leaves, luscious red berries and undemanding nature, all earn it respect. The only real unpleasantness it brings to 'hands on' gardeners is the prickles. But there is so much diversity amongst the numerous cultivars, in leaf variegation and degree of pricklyness, that you will always find one to suit. A key consideration in choosing is the berries. Only a female tree can produce them, but there will need to be a male close enough to pollinate. In all likelihood, there probably is, but *I. a.* 'J. C. van Tol' removes any doubt. Self-pollinating, it gives lots of berries, with lovely shiny, almost completely non-prickly leaves. In stark contrast, with prickles galore is the male silver hedgehog holly, *I. a.* 'Ferox Argentea'. Its white variegation against deep purple stems is echoed in the less prickly female, 'Handsworth New Silver'. 'Madame Briot' and 'Golden Milkboy', both of predictable gender, show a yellow variegation. Actually more shrubby than tree-like are these variegated hollies, and more shrubby still is *I. crenata*, the Japanese holly. Often grown as *I. c.* 'Convexa', it makes an excellent dwarf, prickle-free hedge.

Indigofera (medium shrub)

I. heterantha is a deciduous shrub from open, rocky slopes in the Himalayas. Elegantly formed, and with blue-green leaves delicately divided, it blooms all summer, with dense clusters of purple-pink, pea-like flowers. *I. amblyantha* is similar with bright green leaves, and flowers in shrimp-pink. A close relative of these is *Lespedeza thunbergii*, from Japan and China. It flowers profusely in autumn with dangling heads of rose-purple that weigh down the branches.

Juniperus (small shrub, small tree)

These conifers from various habitats, almost worldwide, are used mainly in gardens as small upright trees or groundcover shrubs. *J. scopulorum*, the Rocky Mountain juniper, is normally grown as cultivars such as 'Skyrocket'. Extremely slender in form, with dense grey-green foliage, this is a hardier, and more diminutive alternative to the Mediterranean cypress (*see* page 52). In complete contrast are low shrubs like *J.* × *pfitzeriana* 'Old Gold', the even lower *J. squamata* 'Blue Carpet' and the really prostrate *J. horizontalis* 'Emerald Spreader'. Dense ground coverers for easy maintenance, they bring important colour to the winter garden.

Koelreutaria (medium tree)

K. paniculata is the golden-rain tree which occurs naturally on poor soils in the Far East. Medium sized with a spreading crown, it is an attractive tree in so many ways. The large divided leaves open pink and turn soft yellow before falling. Large open heads of yellow flowers are produced in July and August, when you won't find many other trees in flower. The fruits that follow are large inflated capsules, tinted pink and red, that hang conspicuously from the branches.

Koelreutaria paniculata.

Laurus nobilis.

Laurus (large shrub, small tree)
L. nobilis is the bay tree from shrubby, rocky places often close to the sea in the Mediterranean region. Easily moulded to shapes by training and pruning – that's how it is typically grown in small gardens. Left untamed, it may get too bulky but would bring the full benefit of the yellow, nectar rich, flower clusters that enliven the dark evergreen aromatic foliage in late winter and spring. The cultivar 'Angustifolia', with narrower leaves, is slightly hardier, and for golden foliage, there is *L. n.* 'Aurea'.

Lavandula (small shrub)
Lavenders are small evergreens, with slender grey-green aromatic leaves and spikes of flowers in the purple-blue-pink range. Classic Mediterranean xerophytes that they are, no self-respecting dry garden could really be without them. And why should it be? The softness, the colour, the scent, the bees; whether a single plant, a splodge of ground cover, or a hedge, lavender brings its own special quality. The traditional English one, *L. angustifolia*, is available in compact cultivars such as 'Hidcote Pink' or the purple 'Hidcote'. 'Loddon Blue' is even

smaller, and the white 'Nana Alba' is distinctly dwarfed. These all flower in mid summer, whereas the French lavender, *L. stoechas*, starts to open its flowers in spring. More intensely fragrant, it has a distinctive purple tuft at the top of each spike. Closely related to lavender, and similar, is *Hyssopus officinalis*, the herb we call hyssop, a low-growing aromatic shrub with spikes of bright blue flowers in summer.

Lavandula stoechas.

Lavatera *'Rosea'*.

Lavatera (medium shrub)
The shrubby mallows we grow in gardens are hybrids and cultivars of Mediterranean plants adapted to rocky coastal places. Woody they are, though in a soft, pithy kind of way, and short-lived, with grey-green leaves that are generally held through winter. Colour is what they give – different shades of pink or white for weeks and weeks in summer. 'Barnsley' has very pale, almost white flowers with a red centre. In 'Rosea' they are deep pink, and 'Candy Floss', pale pink.

Ligustrum (medium shrub, small tree)
These are the privets. Though mainly shrubs of thickets and woodland in the Far East, there is one privet with genuine claims of tree status. *L. lucidum*, the Chinese privet, is a beautiful small tree with glossy evergreen leaves that adorn a neatly formed, rounded crown. Sprays of white flowers are added in late summer, and the rather boastfully named *L. l.* 'Excelsum Superbum' is especially striking with its variegated foliage. These may be sold as large shrubs, rather than trees, but if it's a shrub you want, *L. japonicum* may suit better. Medium sized, dense and upright, it is similar to its cousin in leaf and flower. Famous for hedging, *L. ovalifolium* or *L. vulgare* are the ones most commonly used.

Lonicera (small shrub, medium shrub, climber)
The honeysuckles, from around the globe, are many and varied, but include some evergreens from the Far East that are particularly drought resistant. Two shrubby species, of streamside habitat, are very useful unfussy workaday foliage plants. *L. nitida*, with tiny shiny leaves on arching branches to eye level, is most popular as the cultivar 'Baggesen's Gold' (*see* page 82). *L. pileata*, though common in municipal landscapes, has an appealing simplicity to offer home gardeners. The horizontal branches

Ligustrum lucidum *'Excelsum Superbum'*.

Lonicera japonica *'Aureoreticulata' with a purple* Berberis thunbergii.

create a dense low ground cover, punctuated in spring by fresh emerging leaves. *L. japonica* is a vigorous evergreen climber, often grown for foliage as 'Aureoreticulata' or for flowers as 'Halliana'. They are sweetly scented and all through summer, they open white and turn to yellow. Closely related to the honeysuckles, and just as obliging, are the North American snowberries such as *Symphoricarpus × chenaultii* 'Hancock'. Low spreading and very dense, it is a useful ground cover for difficult places.

Lupinus (medium shrub)
L. arboreus, the tree lupin, comes from dunes and other coastal habitat in California. It is a medium sized, short-lived shrub with finely divided evergreen leaves and clusters of fragrant flowers. Naturally variable from seed, it is normally yellow, but can be blue or white.

Lyonothamnus (small tree)
L. floribundus subsp. *aspleniifolius*, the Catalina ironwood, is a small evergreen tree from dry slopes on some little islands off California. It is quick growing with a graceful slender shape and glossy green leaves, prettily divided like the fronds of a fern – the perfect compliment to its warm peeling red-brown bark. With enough warmth and protection, it may bear large sprays of white flowers early in summer, but is well worth growing anyway.

Mahonia (small shrub)
M. aquifolium, the Oregon grape, is the popular American species. It forms low thickets, to about waist height, in dry open woodland on the West Coast, and is better adapted to drought than the winter flowering Asian species such as *M. × media*. Oregon grape flowers in spring, with dense clusters of rich yellow held above the polished, leathery, evergreen, spiny foliage that will often still be reddish from the winter cold. The blue-black berries that follow are a treat for birds.

Lupinus arboreus.

Mahonia aquifolium.

Myrtus (medium shrub, large shrub)
M. communis, the common myrtle, is a large aromatic evergreen from dry hills around the Mediterranean. Long grown as a flavouring herb and for fruit, its main value in home gardens is from the pretty white flowers, tufted in the centre with fluffy filaments that appear against the deep green leaves in mid-late summer. Purple-black berries follow, drawing further attention to this noble shrub. *M. c.* subsp. *tarentina* is a hardier form which is smaller, to shoulder height, and very free flowering with pink tinged petals and white berries.

Nandina (small shrub, medium shrub)
N. domestica, the heavenly bamboo, is an evergreen shrub from alpine valleys in the Far East. Whilst not exactly relishing dry conditions, it survives well and is a great giver of flower, fruit, foliage and form. Not actually a bamboo at all, but with some of that elegance, its stems rise cane-like from the ground, holding up delicately divided leaves that become red-tinted in the colder months. Then in summer, above the leafy canopy, appear open sprays of white flowers which, in a warm year, turn to glorious red berries that last through winter.

Olea (small tree)
O. europaea is the olive tree, so closely associated with the hot dry summers of its Mediterranean home, that its drought resistance is unquestionable. Not so, its credentials as a hardy garden tree though, but that's what it has become, in the South of England at least. Lacking the heavy denseness

Myrtus communis.

of other broadleaved evergreens, the openness of its rounded crown is accentuated by the silvery grey appearance of the leathery leaves. Gnarled branches with rugged bark further enrich the character, and because olive trees really don't ever get very big, they're perfect in Mediterranean courtyard gardens, and you may even get olives. Similar but much hardier is *Phillyria latifolia*, sometimes called the green olive. It produces a beautiful rounded open crown of shiny dark green leaves

Olearia (medium shrub, large shrub)
These are the daisy bushes, from Australia and New Zealand. They are all evergreens, typically with white undersides to the leaves, and profuse displays of little daisy flowers. The medium sized rounded *O.* × *haastii* and the taller, slightly prickly *O. macrodonta* each have white summer flowers and are two of the hardiest. Less hardy, but grown for their profuse spring flowering, are *O. phlogopappa* and its hybrid *O.* × *scilloniensis*. These have given rise to cultivars, such as *O. p.* 'Comber's Pink' and the blue *O.* × *s.* 'Master Michael'.

Ostrya (medium tree)
O. carpinifolia, the hop hornbeam, occurs naturally on dry and stony hillsides around the Mediterranean, and makes an attractive round-headed, medium sized garden tree. Its beauty lies in the simple pleasures it gives: long pendulous yellow catkins and bright green leaves in spring, a neat shape and white, hop-like fruit clusters in summer that turn soft brown with the yellow autumn leaves. The common hornbeam we use for hedging is *Carpinus betulus*. Its cultivar 'Fastigiata' is neatly cone-shaped, and is something special as a specimen tree.

Ozothamnus (small shrub, medium shrub)
These tiny leaved evergreens from open rocky places in Tasmania certainly look and feel at home in the dry garden. The medium sized *O. rosmarinifolius* and the smaller *O. ledifolius* are both fairly hardy, with heads of white flowers that open from reddish coloured buds in early summer. The silvery leaves of *O. r.* 'Silver Jubilee' are an additional attraction, found also in the closely related, aromatic curry plant, *Helichrysum italicum* subsp. *serotinum*.

Parthenocissus quinquefolia.

Parthenocissus (climber)
P. quinquefolia, from eastern North America, is called Virginia creeper, and *P. tricuspidata*, Boston ivy, though it is from China and Japan. They are both vigorous, deciduous woody climbers from woods and rocky slopes and have attractively shaped foliage with superb autumn colour. Small grape-like fruits are produced when the summer is hot and dry enough. Indeed the grape vine, *Vitis vinifera*, is closely related and available in decorative forms such as the coloured leaved *V. v.* 'Purpurea'.

Perovskia (small shrub)
P. atriplicifolia is Russian sage from open rocky places in the mountains of Afghanistan through to Tibet. Slender stems, white in colour, arise each year from its woody base. They bear grey-green, somewhat feathery leaves and are topped off, for several weeks in late summer, by sprays of lavender-blue flowers at about waist height.

Perovskia atriplicifolia.

Philadelphus (small shrub, medium shrub)

P. coronarius is the strong growing deciduous shrub, mock orange. From dry rocky hills in southern and eastern Europe, it has been bred with species of similar habitats in Texas and Mexico, to produce some wonderful sweetly scented, pure white or creamy flowering shrubs. 'Belle Etoile' is an early variety, medium sized and very fragrant with maroon markings at the centre of each bloom. 'Manteau d'Hermine' is a small shrub with equally fragrant, double flowers a little later in June/July. *Carpenteria californica* is a very showy evergreen relative for hot sunny places. Medium sized, with glossy green leaves, it bears large white yellow-centred flowers in mid-summer.

Phlomis (small shrub)

P. fruticosa, the Jerusalem sage, is a small, mound forming evergreen shrub from cliffs and rocky places around the Mediterranean. It has velvety grey-green leaves and bright yellow flowers that occur in whorls, wrapped around the stems in summer. Other shrubby species such as *P. italica*, are a little less hardy but there are much tougher ones amongst the herbaceous perennials.

Phlomis italica.

Photinia × fraseri.

Phygelius × rectus 'Moonraker'.

Photinia (medium shrub, large shrub, small tree)
From woodlands and hillsides in the Far East, it is the evergreen photinias that are most drought resistant. It's mainly for the reddish colours in their young leaves that they are grown, and one cultivar in particular is the chosen one: *P. × fraseri* 'Red Robin'. You see it everywhere with glossy green leaves, brilliant red when young and sometimes, following a hot summer the previous year, with large heads of white flowers in spring. Another large shrub, *P. davidiana*, boasts bunches of bright red berries, but is usually seen as the cultivar 'Palette', with leaves rather dubiously blotched pink and white. Closely allied to photinia is *Aronia arbutifolia*, a medium sized deciduous shrub grown for spring flowers, autumn leaf colour and edible berries. Though naturally from moist habitats in America, this and other chokeberries show good drought resistance in gardens.

Phygelius (small shrub)
P. capensis is the Cape figwort from the mountains of Natal. It often grows by streams and thrives on the moisture, but it is fairly drought tolerant once established in gardens. Grown for its large open heads of drooping, orangey-red, trumpet-shaped flowers in summer, it is a small evergreen shrub which can actually get quite large, and unruly, in warm sunny spots. Slightly more tender is *P. aequalis* and the hybrid *P. × rectus*, which has given rise to some excellent garden cultivars such as 'Moonraker'. Though small shrubs in southern England,

they may behave more like herbaceous perennials where it's colder.

Phyllostachys (medium shrub, tall shrub)
These bamboos form groves in moist open woodland and streamsides in the Far East. They make tall handsome evergreen plants, growing to head height or a lot more, and are normally fairly well behaved in terms of their spread. *P. nigra*, the black bamboo and *P. aurea*, the golden one are both fairly drought resistant as far as bamboos go, and *P. n.* var. *henonis* is particularly so.

Physocarpus (medium shrub)
P. opulifolius, or ninebark, is a deciduous shrub that forms thickets on rocky slopes and stream banks in eastern North America. White, slightly pinkish flowers appear in clusters along its arching stems in early summer. Reddish fruits follow, and peeling bark brings winter interest but it's the two coloured leaved cultivars that really make it popular: 'Diabolo' has dark purple foliage while in 'Dart's Gold' the young leaves are bright yellow. Good foliage colours, and flowers, also occur amongst cultivars of the closely related small shrub *Spiraea japonica*.

Physocarpus opulifolius
'*Diabolo*'.

Pinus (small shrubs, small trees, medium trees)
Occurring widely throughout the Northern Hemisphere, many pines originate from dry rocky mountainsides or other arid environments. They are characterful evergreens, often with interestingly spreading crowns, fine foliage texture, richly coloured bark and attractive cones. Not all would suit small gardens, but one that does is the Italian stone pine, *P. pinea*, a small, flat topped tree which captures the spirit of the Mediterranean just as well as the cypress (*see* page 52) with which it contrasts perfectly. It is great for pine nuts, as is *P. cembre*, the Swiss stone pine – a medium sized tree maintaining a formal column shape clothed with dark blue-green needles and blue cones. Also from the Alps is *P. mugo* – a small tree normally grown in a shrubby form such as *P. m.* 'Ophir', which has warm yellow winter foliage. For the Chinese willow pattern look, choose *P. parviflora*, often treated as a bonsai in Japanese gardens. And not to ignore

Pittosporum '*Tom Thumb*'.

Pittosporum *'Garnettii'*.

the Americans, though most are too large for home gardens, *P. patula* from Mexico is a small elegant tree with reddish bark, spreading branches and slender drooping bright green needles.

Pittosporum (small shrub, medium shrub, large shrub)
P. tenuifolium is a large evergreen shrub of woodland in New Zealand. One of the hardiest of the genus, it is grown for the pale green and shiny wavy-edged leaves that sit prettily on black stems, but there are coloured-leaved cultivars that attract more attention. 'Irene Paterson' is notable for having young leaves that emerge creamy white, becoming greener later and pink tinged in winter. It is a small rounded shrub, as is 'Tom Thumb', one of the few evergreens we can grow with purple leaves that are not long and strap shaped. *P.* 'Garnettii' is large and conically shaped, with creamy-margined, grey-green leaves. The Japanese mock orange, *P. tobira*, is a medium-large, slow growing evergreen of rocky coastal hills and sandy seashores. Well suited to warm seaside gardens, it has distinctive, glossy deep green foliage and clusters of lusciously scented, creamy white flowers in late spring.

Poncirus (large shrub)
P. trifoliata is the bitter orange, from wooded hills in the Far East. A large, slow growing, decidu-

ous shrub of rounded shape, its stiff green stems are armed, somewhat alarmingly, with really long sharp spines. Showy, fragrant white, 'orange-blossom' flowers are produced in late spring, followed by small green 'oranges' that ripen to yellow before converting to marmalade.

Potentilla fruticosa *'Primrose Beauty'*.

Potentilla (small shrub, medium shrub)

P. fruticosa is the shrubby cinquefoil, a deciduous shrub of damp rocky places across the colder parts of the Northern Hemisphere. Its small finely divided leaves emerge early in spring, on a tangle of wiry stems that later carry rose-like flowers over much of summer. Colour and size depend on the cultivar, and there are many to choose from. 'Elizabeth' captures the general spirit, with relatively large yellow flowers on a small dome shaped shrub from late spring through to autumn. 'Primrose Beauty' has grey-green foliage, but really silvery foliage is a feature of some, such as the white flowered 'Manchu'. Oranges, pinks and red flowers occur too but tend to fade in hot sun. Most make good dwarf hedges, and some such as 'Friedrichsenii' come up to eye level or more.

Prostanthera

P. cuneata is the alpine mint bush from open woods and heathland in the mountains of south-east Australia and Tasmania. It is a low evergreen shrub with tiny, glossy, green, aromatic leaves and small white tubular summer flowers, marked inside with purple and yellow. Other mint bushes, such as the taller and very flowery *P. rotundifolia*, are only to be relied on in warmer gardens.

Prunus (small shrub, large shrub, small tree)

From this enormous genus of mainly trees, there are two evergreen shrubs amongst the most drought resistant. From rocky hills in south-east Europe and near Asia, is the cherry laurel, *P. laurocerasus*, and the Portuguese laurel, *P. lusitanica*, is from a little further west. Each has large glossy leaves and slender heads of small white flowers, most conspicuous in the slightly later, June flowering Portuguese species. Big and bulky, their main use is hedging, but there are some more compact cultivars of cherry laurel for decorative schemes in smaller gardens. *P. l.* 'Otto Luyken' is one such shrub with slender leaves of really dark green that make the perfect foil for the abundant spring flowering. Also small but deciduous is *P. × cistena*, with white spring flowers against reddish-purple leaves. One of its parents is the purple leaved plum, *P. cerasifera* 'Pissardii' – similar in colour but a small tree and good for hedging. *P. tenella* 'Firehill', another small shrub, is a form of dwarf Russian almond, while the small tree, *P. dulcis*, is the almond of commerce but excellent too for early spring blossom.

Prunus laurocerasus *'Otto Luyken'*.

Prunus tenella *'Fire hill'*
with Phormium *'Platts Black'.*

Pyracantha (medium shrub)

These are the firethorns, of rocky hillsides and woodland edge, from southern Europe eastwards to China. They are densely branched evergreen, spiny shrubs, with white flowers in early summer and then showy displays of red, orange or yellow berries – that's the order in which they are favoured by birds, so you choose between late winter colour and happy wildlife. They are easy to grow apart from one thing, Pyracantha scab (*see* page 146), which can ruin the fruiting display. A group of cultivars, called the Saphyr range, has been especially selected for their resistance to this.

Rhamnus (large shrub)

R. alaternus, the Italian buckthorn, is from dry shrubby places around the Mediterranean. It is a large fast growing evergreen with yellowy flowers of little interest but, after a warm enough summer, fine displays of red berries. In gardens it is grown mainly as *R. a.* 'Argenteovariegata', with leaves of grey green margined creamy-white. *R. cathartica* is the common buckthorn, a large spiny deciduous shrub that is great for wildlife. Related to these is Christ's thorn, *Paliurus spina-christi*, a large shrub of dry hills from southern Europe to China, which has curious, large, round, woody fruits.

Rhus (large shrub)

R. typhina is the stag's horn sumach of dry stony soils and other habitats in North America. It is a large deciduous shrub that can form dense thickets of suckers, especially if disturbed at its roots. But hopefully it will grow like a little tree, with an open, spreading crown of thick furry branches that form a curly winter sculpture, decorated by crimson fruits if it's a female plant, then in spring sprout large divided leaves that eventually turn to all the brilliant colours of autumn. *R. glabra*, the smooth sumach, is similar but without the fur. Attractive feathery leaved forms are available from both species, none better though than the hybrid cultivar *R.* × *pulvinata* 'Red Autumn Lace'. *Cotinus coggygria*, the smoke bush, is closely related to sumach. It occurs on rocky hills from central Europe through to China and is commonly grown in a coloured leaved form such as 'Royal purple'.

Robinia (tall shrub, small tree, medium tree)

R. pseudoacacia, the black locust from America, occurs commonly as a wild tree in Europe. Large, fast growing and thorny, often suckering from the roots, and notoriously brittle of branch, it is not an obvious choice despite its finely textured foliage and clusters of fragrant white flowers in summer. But there is one cultivar of particular value as a garden tree – *R. p.* 'Frisia' is slower growing and not so tall, with leaves of golden yellow from their emergence in spring right through to autumn. A smaller tree, ideal for a dry courtyard, is the distinctively round headed *R. p.* 'Inermis', grown

Robinia pseudoacacia
'*Frisia*'.

Robinia hispida.

for foliage only, unlike the shrubby *R. hispida*, in which large heads of flowers feature strongly in early summer.

Romneya (medium shrub)

R. coulteri is the tree poppy, of dry rocky ground in California and Mexico. From an ever widening woody base, it grows anew each year with grey green elegantly divided foliage topped with fat promising buds. Then fried egg-like, in size and colour, but delicately fragrant and fragile, the blooms appear repeatedly through summer. *R. c.* 'White Cloud' has just a little bit more of everything – vigour of growth, blueness of leaf and flower size.

Rosa banksiae *'Lutea'*.

Rosa (small shrub, medium shrub, climber)
The big bloomy hybrids of rose beds are not very drought resistant. They've been bred for other qualities, but some of the natural rose species are adapted to dry habitats. They don't look like the latest offerings in the rose catalogues, but they certainly offer a simpler charm. *R. rugosa* (*see* page 130) from sandy shores in the Far East, is a small but vigorous shrub, with lush green foliage, pinkish-red flowers through summer and big rounded bright red hips. From similar habitat in Europe is the Scotch rose, *R. pimpinellifolia*. It has delicate, finely textured foliage and lots of small white flowers in early summer followed by dark purplish hips. *R. virginiana* is an American species of coastal habitat with bright pink flowers, glistening red hips and glossy green foliage turning to wonderful autumn colours. They are all small suckering prickly shrubs, but don't hold that against them. *R. glauca* is medium sized and neither suckering nor very prickly. It comes from mountain regions in Europe and has arching stems with leaves which are purplish in the sun and greyish in the shade. Either way, they are a good foil for the deep pink and white flowers. Roses are often propagated by budding, but these species would be better on their own roots if you can find them that way. If it's a climber you want, for a warm sunny wall, try the late-spring flowering *R. banksiae*, from China. Almost thornless and evergreen, it is normally grown as the double yellow *R. b.* 'Lutea'.

Salvia officinalis *'Icterina'*.

Rosmarinus (small shrub, medium shrub)
R. officinalis is the herb rosemary, from dry shrubby coastal areas around the Mediterranean. Fairly upright to about shoulder height but spreading a little, its branches are adorned with tiny, slender, aromatic evergreen leaves (*see* page 16). Little pale blue flowers first open in the bleakest winter months and continue until early summer. Various cultivars introduce different shapes and flower colours. *R. o.* 'Severn Sea' is low and spreading with bright blue flowers. 'Mrs Jessopp's Upright' has flowers of the natural colour, and 'Roseus' is the normal shape with pink flowers.

Ruta (small shrub)
R. graveolens, from dry rocky places in southern Europe, is the common rue, a small evergreen shrub forming a mound of soft stems and pungently aromatic leaves. Clusters of yellow flowers appear in summer but detract slightly from the lacy pattern of the blue green foliage. *R. g.* 'Jackman's Blue' is the one to grow, as it is more compact and vivid in foliage colour.

Salvia (small shrub)

S. officinalis is the herb sage of dry stony soils around the Mediterranean. From a woody base, it forms a low spreading evergreen mound with heads of purple-blue flowers in summer, but it's mainly the foliage that we grow it for. Grey-green in the species, there are coloured leaved forms such as the softly tinted 'Purpurascens' and variegated 'Icterina', which are grown more for decoration than for cooking. Other shrubby salvias from dry habitats in Mexico will survive winter outside in warm sheltered gardens. The many cultivars of *S. greggii*, *S. microphylla*, and their hybrid *S.* × *jamensis*, bring brightly coloured flower displays through late summer and autumn. (Other, non-woody, salvias are described on page 117)

Sambucus nigra *'Black Beauty'*.

Sambucus (medium shrub, tall shrub)

S. nigra is the common elder, a large deciduous shrub growing in a range of conditions from Scandinavia down to North Africa and western Asia. Its black berries are loved by birds, and there is a red-berried one too, *S. racemosa*, whose range extends across to Siberia. If it's the berries you want, and the heads of little white flowers, they are best left alone in a wildish part of the garden. However, both species are normally grown in different forms with coloured foliage, and pruned hard each spring (*see* page 147) *S. r.* 'Sutherland Gold' has feathery-edged leaves that are some contrast with the darkness of *S. n.* 'Black Beauty'. Closely related is the medium sized Mediterranean evergreen *Viburnum tinus*, grown for its clusters of small white flowers through winter.

Santolina pinnata *subsp.* neapolitana *'Edward Bowles'*.

Santolina (small shrub)

S. chamaecyparissus, the cotton lavender is a low mound-forming evergreen of Mediterranean cliffs and rocky slopes, grown for its finely textured silvery foliage. The flowers in July and August appear as little yellow buttons, so if the silver/yellow combination offends, choose *S. rosmarinifolia*, with leaves of lush green, or the grey-green foliage and creamy flowers of *S. pinnata* subsp. *neapolitana* 'Edward Bowles'.

Sophora (small tree, medium tree)
S. japonica, from China actually, is the Japanese pagoda tree. Similar to the black locust (*see* page 71) in size, foliage, and flower, it blooms later, in August, and holds its leaves longer into autumn. *S. j.* 'Pendula' is a weeping form which is unlikely to flower, but it makes a good alternative to a weeping willow if the soil is really dry. There are also some exotic looking evergreen species of Sophora from the Southern Hemisphere. *S. tetraptera* and *S. microphylla* are both small trees with beautifully fine textured foliage and drooping clusters of rich yellow flowers in Spring.

Tamarix (large shrub)
The tamarisks are large deciduous shrubs, highly adapted to growing in sandy and stony places near the sea in Europe and Asia. They have a distinctive look, with slender arching branches and feathery foliage forming great plumes that become pink and frothy to the extreme when the tiny flowers open. This happens in spring on *T. tetrandra*, which you prune after flowering, and in late summer on *T. ramosissima*, pruned in late winter (*see* page 147). It's important, this pruning, if the potential for elegance is not to turn out as unruly chaos.

Taxus (small tree)
T. baccata, from Europe, West Asia and North Africa, is the common yew of English churchyards and formal garden hedges. Amongst the numerous cultivars of this species are some small, slow growing, evergreen trees, grown for their shape, foliage texture and colour. The solid upright presence of Irish yew, *T. b.* 'Fastigiata', comes over somewhat more cheery in the cultivar 'Fastigiata Aurea'. *T. b.* 'Dovastoniana' also has a yellow leaved form, but its branches extend horizontally and the leafy stems hang down to give it a more informal appearance.

Tamarix tetrandra.

Taxus baccata *'Fastigiata Aurea'*.

Teucrium (small shrub)

T. fruticans is the shrubby germander from rocky places near the Mediterranean. It has white, stiffly arching stems and silvery leaves, forming an ever-green mound to waist height. Small pale blue flow-ers appear through summer, and in *T. f.* 'Azureum' they are a good dark blue. *T. chamaedrys* (wall ger-mander) is a much smaller green leaved Mediter-ranean evergreen, with rose-pink summer flowers.

Trachycarpus fortunei.

Trachycarpus (small tree)

T. fortunei, from China, is the chusan palm – the hardiest palm tree there is. It grows outside in most parts of the UK and though, admittedly, not the most glamorous palm, it does create that look that only a palm tree can. The single trunk is clad with the coarse fibrous remains of old leaves, but if its shagginess offends, they can be stripped away for a more groomed look. Growing quite tall eventually, but only slowly, it remains a small tree for most of us, with enormous fan-shaped evergreen leaves that sprout in a cluster from the very top. Large sprays of yellow flowers appear in early summer from amongst the leaves, but they are really just interesting accessories. Another fairly hardy fan-leaved palm, and more drought resistant still, is the shrubby Mediterranean *Chamaerops humilis*.

Wisteria sinensis.

Wisteria (climber)

W. sinensis is a vigorous tree climber from China, but it can be reasonably tamed against walls and other structures. With large divided deciduous leaves, it produces enormous drooping flower heads in early summer. Fragrant and normally a soft purplish-blue, they are clear white in *W. s.* 'Alba'. The Japanese species, *W. floribunda*, is a bit less vigorous but no less stunning, with cultivars in a wide range of colours, and often with flower heads as long as your arm.

Yucca gloriosa.

Yucca (small shrub, medium shrub)

These dramatic looking evergreens, with bold strap-shaped leaves, and giant heads of nodding white summer flowers, come from extreme, sandy habitats in North and Central America. Of the frost hardy species, *Y. gloriosa* is the one to really catch the desert look, with its leaf rosettes supported on a stout branching trunk to head height. But beware, for its common name, Spanish dagger, doesn't belie the viciousness of its spiny leaf tips. Hardier still is the low growing branchless *Y. filamentosa*, with white wispy threads around its leaves. Good variegated forms are available of each of these species. *Beschorneria yuccoides*, from Mexico, is a fairly hardy close relative and a definite yucca look-alike. Its bluish-green fleshy leaves form a tight rosette, above which appear drooping green and red flowers early in summer.

Beschorneria yuccoides.

NON-WOODY PLANTS

Perennials

Most perennials are herbaceous, dying back to the ground each winter, though the list here does include some evergreens. The need for perennials to grow back again does make extra demands on water, but the ones listed are able to cope with that, and a garden without them would miss so much – fresh new shoots appearing from nowhere, offering textures and shapes not seen in woody plants. Some start really early, flowering in the winter or spring, under the canopy of trees and shrubs. Others come later, flowering in summer or autumn, and normally expecting a sunnier spot.

There is such a wide range of perennials, even amongst the more drought resistant species. Large leafy flowery ones often have deep taproots to support their extravagance, while the low creepers usually have smaller leaves and fibrous roots. There are the woodland perennials too, finding ways to cope with drought and shade, and then grasses and bulbs can be thrown into the mix. You can go for the manicured well-tended border or

Hardy annuals – sweet, simple and smiley.

Grasses, such as miscanthus, *are one type of perennial that contributes well to the winter garden.*

you can plant wild perennials in rough grass and under trees. The water-efficient garden solution is normally somewhere between, matching the right plants to the appropriate place for an informal look that requires minimal interference or watering.

Hardy annuals, biennials and half-hardy annuals

Also with non-woody stems are those plants we grow for their flowers, and once the display is over, they die. Annuals flower in their first year; biennials wait till the second, but succumb they will to the frenzy of flowering, leaving only seed as potential for re-growth. With hardy annuals and biennials, the next generation may well appear of its own accord, but with the more exotic half-hardy annuals, you will need to buy replacements or go to a good deal of effort to grow them. What they all give you is flowers, lots of them, plus all the fun and excitement of seeing the garden change from season to season and year to year.

The simplicity of hardy annuals, and the quick return they offer, makes them great for encouraging kids to garden, but why stop there? For the price of a packet of seed you get dozens of plants, flowering for weeks – pot marigolds, candytuft, love-in-a-mist, sunflowers. They might not be rare and exotic, but they do have natural beauty and traditional charm that can only serve to enrich our gardens. You can buy them as single species, often with mixed colours, or even as mixes of species. Hardy annuals sown directly into the ground in spring will bring new and vibrant colour into the garden throughout the summer.

Salvia farinacea *'Victoria'. But is it worth the extra water? Probably.*

Biennials together – cotton thistle and foxglove like to self-seed.

Grown for spring bedding, biennials are planted out in autumn, but most could be sown direct early one year for flowering the next. The plants listed here include true biennials that naturally die after flowering, and others such as wallflowers, that could live on, but which we normally discard.

Neither hardy annuals nor biennials would need much watering at all. You can normally rely on the weather to help you out, sooner or later with autumn plantings, and sowing direct is always a good water saving method (*see* page 127). Many biennials are natural looking plants suited to wilder parts of a garden, where their self-seeding eliminates the need for planting each year. Left undisturbed in this way, they grow taproots, deep into the ground, storing food to give strength for flowering, and ensuring survival through dry periods.

As far as water guzzling is concerned, half-hardy annuals are a different matter, and only those from really hot dry natural habitats are included here. These are the ones we grow from seed under glass, or buy from the garden centre, and plant out as summer bedding after the danger of frost has passed. This brings exotic new colour to the garden each year, but it's not the most water-efficient way to go about things. Problems arise, not just from hot dryness at the time of planting, but also from the obstruction it causes to plants that want to produce deep searching roots. Some, such as annual cosmos, may be branded as half-hardy, but can actually be treated as hardy, and sown direct, to overcome this difficulty. Others, such as Livingstone daisy, with really effective water saving leaves, can be planted out with little concern.

Acaena saccaticupula *'Blue Haze'*.

Acaena (perennial)

The different species of New Zealand burr occur mainly on dry stony river beds and open grassland. They are low evergreen, spreading ground coverers that form mats of attractively divided foliage from which arise flowers that turn to bristly spherical seed heads. Two coloured leaved forms are particularly effective; *A. microphylla* 'Copper Carpet' and *A. saccaticupula* 'Blue Haze'.

Achillea (perennial)

A. millefolium, or yarrow, is a feathery leaved, spreading perennial that occurs in dry grassy places throughout Europe and Asia. Its green persistence, in the brown lawns of high summer, is testament to its drought tolerance. The white flowered species is good for the wild garden, but there are excellent colour forms including lilacs, deep pinks and curious rusty oranges, all to about knee height and flowering through summer. *Achillea filipendulina* is a taller plant, of wetter grassy places and streamsides in western and central Asia. It is usually grown as a cultivar, such as 'Gold Plate' with large flat heads of golden yellow. Much smaller, forming low mats of grey-green foliage with bright yellow flowers, is *A. tomentosa* from dry hills in south-west Europe.

Achillea millefolium *'Terracotta'*.

Agapanthus africanus.

Agastache rugosa *'Liquorice Blue' backed by* Lonicera nitida *'Baggesen's Gold'*.

Agapanthus (perennials)

These South African perennials form clumps of strap shaped leaves with rounded heads of flowers in various shades of blue or white. The larger evergreen species, such as *A. africanus*, come from coastal areas; they are the most drought tolerant but least hardy. Deciduous forms, typified by *A. campanulatus*, tend to have narrower leaves and smaller flower heads over a shorter period in mid-late summer. They come from moist mountain grasslands but do show good drought resistance once established.

Agastache (perennial)

A. foeniculum is the anise hyssop, of dry fields and shrubby places through many parts of North America. Sturdy upright stems, to waist height, bear aromatic edible foliage and, in the latter part of summer, dense vertical, fuzzy textured spikes of purple flowers. *A. rugosa*, or Korean mint, from mountains in the Far East, has a similar look and flavour. Good seed strains are available, such as 'Liquorice blue', which flower in their first year from sowing.

Agrostemma (hardy annual)

A. githago is the corn cockle. Native to the Mediterranean region but widely naturalized, it was once a common weed of arable land. Its slender, narrow leaved stems, sometimes to waist height, hold up large magenta flowers with elegant poise. Grown

Agrostemma githago
'Milas'.

in rich soil on their own, the plants need support, so they often look best mingling amongst a cornfield mix. *A. g.* 'Milas' is softer in colour, and the related *Silene coeli-rosa* is smaller altogether, in a wide colour range.

Alcea (biennial, perennial)
Probably originating as a cultivated plant in southwestern Asia, *A. rosea* is the hollyhock of old English cottage gardens. Growing to head height and more, the distinguished spires of flowers, single or double, are borne in a wide range of colours, from yellow to the darkest maroon. It is actually a short lived perennial, but so prone it is to rust disease, that biennial cultivation works best. *A. ficifolia*, from Siberia is similar in appearance but a bit less susceptible to rust. *A. r.* 'Chater's Double', and the single flowered *A. f.* 'Happy Lights', are good colour mixes but if they're just too pretty for you, try the single flowered, almost black, *A. rosea* 'Black Knight'.

Alchemilla (perennial)
A. mollis is the lady's mantle of woodland and stream banks in Eastern Europe and near Asia. Carefree self-seeding and general unfussiness give it a casual presence in many gardens, but it has a modest comfortable beauty. The large round soft green leaves hold raindrops like shiny jewels, and then fluffy summer flower sprays of greenish yellow blend perfectly with the foliage. It makes broad clumps to about shin height, while *A. erythropoda*, from alpine meadows, is half the size with spent flowers turning reddish tints.

Alcea rosea.

Allium christophii *with*
Alchemilla mollis.

Allium (perennials)
Mainly bulbs as they are, onions are widespread across the Northern Hemisphere, but the most ornamental species are from dry habitats in Central Asia. Spherical purplish heads rise proudly in early-mid summer, by which time in some species the strap-shaped leaves have already withered. *A. cristophii* is like this; its really large spheres, to about knee height, are open and starry with a sculptural quality that lasts well into the seed head stage. 'Globemaster' is taller, with denser heads of deep violet, while *A.* × *hollandicum* 'Purple Sensation' is taller still. The little herb chives is *A. schoenoprasum*, no mean plant when it comes to pretty flowers (*see* page 138), and for something completely different, if pretty is not entirely your thing, try the onion relative *Nectaroscordum siculum*. Intriguing though slightly sinister, its flowers hang down, fleshy coloured with a tint of green.

Amaranthus (hardy annual, half-hardy annual)
A. caudatus, or love-lies-bleeding, is a tropical grain crop that also grows wild by roadsides in Asia, Africa, and South America. However, its extraordinary bunches of long red flowering tassels give it special distinction in gardens, where it is normally bedded out after the frosts have passed. Much more water efficient however, if sown direct, and if you wait until May, when the soil is really warm, there's still plenty of time for it to grow up and flower that summer. It usually reaches around waist height, getting dangly when fully laden with flowers. *A. hypochondriacus* is much more upright and flowers really quickly from seed in the dwarf, purple-leaved cultivar 'Pygmy Torch'. *Atriplex hortensis* var. *rubra* is a hardier cousin of these. Far less dramatic in flower, but with rich reddish leaves, it'll pop up happily amongst other plants once introduced.

Amaranthus hypochondriacus.

Anchusa capensis *'Blue Angel'*.

Anchusa (hardy annual, perennial)

A. capensis is the summer forget-me-not, of dry sandy places in South Africa. It's blue, white centred flowers, are tiny, but there are masses of them, from mid-summer to autumn. 'Blue Angel' is compact, to shin height, and there are mixed strains too with pinks and whites included. *A. azurea* is a short lived perennial, from dry grassland and stony hills in the Mediterranean region and Eastwards. In June, from a tuft of coarse hairy leaves, it produces upright heads, of really true blue flowers. 'Little John' grows to knee height while 'Loddon Royalist' is twice as tall, but with sturdy stems and a strong vibrant colour.

Anthemis (perennial)

A. punctata subsp. *cupaniana* is a low spreading perennial of cliffs and rocky hillsides in Sicily. Its silver-grey, lacy leaves are the perfect foil for the large, long lasting, white daisies that appear above them in early summer. *A. tinctoria* is another European from similar habitats, with fresh green lacy foliage to knee height. Flowering extravagantly through mid-summer, in yellow of one shade or another, does sometimes spell its demise, but cutting back as soon as the flurry is over will help it recover. A close relative of these is chamomile (*Chamaemelum nobile*), which in the form 'Treneague' is often used to create fragrant lawns.

Anthemis tinctoria
'E.C. Buxton'.

Anthriscus sylvestris.

Anthriscus (biennial)

A. sylvestris is the common cow parsley of grassy places in Europe, North Africa and parts of Asia. Also called Queen Anne's Lace, all its visible parts are loose and open. The frothy white flowers in May, at about waist height, provide important food for wildlife and it self-seeds prolifically. If the natural species is just a bit too wild looking, try *A. s.* 'Ravenswing' with bronze coloured foliage and pinky white flowers.

Aquilegia (perennial)

The columbines, with their delicately divided foliage, and distinctive nodding flowers, are found in open woods and shaded rocky places throughout the northern hemisphere. Flowering late in spring, they may die back if the summer gets dry, but return the following year, even if only from self-sown seed, a fragile presence that matches their dainty appearance. *A. Canadensis* (red columbine) has bicoloured flowers of yellow and red to about knee height. *A. longissima* (longspur columbine) is another North American of similar height with yellow flowers. Breeding these with the European *A. vulgaris* (Granny's bonnet) has produced the popular McKana hybrids and other garden strains. Of similar natural habitat is the closely related European, *Thalictrum aquilegifolium*. It looks similar too, until the fluffy purple or white flowers appear.

Aubrieta × cultorum.

Arabis (perennial)

A. caucasica, or rock cress, grows on rocks and cliffs in south-east Europe and western Asia. Its low evergreen mats of greyish leaves become covered in spring, with little white scented flowers. 'Flora Pleno' is a good double flowered form, and there are pinks and reds available too. *Aubrieta × cultorum*, mainly in shades of purple and the bright yellow *Aurinia saxatilis* (alyssum) are closely related and similar in many ways. Together, these three create solid clumps and mats of colour, on walls, rockeries and the edge of beds. It is hard to imagine spring without them.

Armeria maritima *and*
Armeria maritima *'Alba'*.

Armeria (perennial)

A. maritima, from western Europe, is the low, ground hugging evergreen we call thrift. It occurs wild in salt marshes, coastal cliffs, pastures and mountains. The soft cushions of grassy leaves burst into life in late spring when bobbles of reddish, pink or white flowers appear over the top of them. *A. pseudarmeria*, from coastal grassland in Portugal, is similar looking but chunkier, with much broader leaves and flowers to knee height. *A. juniperifolia*, at the other extreme, is a diminutive alpine.

Artemesia (perennial)

Continuing the silvery theme (from page 44) are the following two herbaceous species. *A. stelleri-ana* is from coastal dunes and cliffs in north-east Asia. Grown in gardens as the low carpeting *A. s. 'Boughton Silver'*, it has the typical lacy leaves of artemesia though more chunkily cut than most. The American prairie plant, *A. ludoviciana*, is normally seen as the cultivar 'Silver Queen' which forms spreading clumps to above knee height. The herb, tarragon, is *A. dracunculus*.

Asparagus (perennial)

A. officinalis is the vegetable we eat. From sandy soils near the sea, and by river banks in western Europe, it is a dense clump-forming perennial with

Artemisia ludoviciana *'Silver Queen'*.

deep fleshy roots. The stems rise to head height bearing feathery leaf-like structures that give a light airy effect. Black or red berries occur on female plants but it is normally grown for the young shoots, fatter and juicier on male cultivars especially chosen for eating.

Asphodeline lutea.

Asphodeline (perennial)

A. lutea, the yellow asphodel, comes from dry rocky fields and mountainsides around the Mediterranean. Its blue-green tufts of leaves have the look of a grass plant, but when the flowers rise, sometimes to shoulder height, in late spring, it becomes clear that it isn't. Attractive seed capsules follow, sustaining the vertical line that the plant creates. Of

similar origin is *Asphodelus albus* with white flowers held up not quite so high.

Aster divarcatus.

Aster (perennial)

Mainly from North America, and including the Michaelmas daisies, there are a couple of species from dry open ground and woodlands that are particularly useful. With lots of little white daisy flowers in late summer and autumn, *A. divarcatus* has lax black stems that look best if allowed to flop over other, earlier flowering plants. *A. ericoides* comes in blues, pinks and whites, and in the more compact cultivars, such as 'Blue Star', it shouldn't need staking. Another fairly drought resistant species, growing to just above knee height, but with much larger flowers, is *A. × frikartii*. It is a Eura-

Aster × frikartii *'Monch'*.

sian hybrid, and in the cultivar 'Monch' blooms for weeks and weeks on sturdy stems. A close relative of all these is *Boltonia asteroides*, another American species, flowering late in the season to knee height, with small white or purplish daisies.

Ballota (perennial)
B. pseudodictamnus is a very silvery leaved evergreen from rocky places on Crete and thereabouts. From quite a woody base, most of the growth is soft, building up into a dense tangle of stems and leaves with little pinkish white flowers in early summer. If pruned hard each spring it looks tidier, forming neat, woolly white mounds, to knee height.

Baptisia (perennial)
B. australis is the false, or wild, indigo from the south-eastern USA. It grows in wooded or grassy areas forming deep searching roots and prettily divided soft green foliage that holds well through to autumn. Long vertical open heads of loosely arranged, deep blue flowers up to shoulder height, provide the main display in early summer.

Bellis (biennial)
B. perennis is the common daisy of lawns and pastures in northern Europe. As pretty as it is, you wouldn't plant it in gardens, but there are double flowered cultivars, such as in Tasso Series, that cheer up our gardens in spring with their bobble

Bellis perennis *'Tasso Strawberries and Cream'*.

heads of pink, white or red – perennial of course, but used as for spring bedding.

Bergenia (perennial)
Elephant's ears are evergreen perennials from moist shaded rocky places and cliffs in Siberia and the Himalayas. Thick woody stems at the soil surface spread slowly to form chunky clumps of large rounded glossy leaves. Dense clusters of flowers in reds, pinks or whites crop up, in spring, amongst the foliage, which in many forms turns to bronze or reddish winter tints. But for some, the leaves are

too 'cabbagey' and the pinks too rude, so check the lists, and your heart's desire, with caution. Extreme sunny dryness can be a problem but, if tolerated, it will yield the best possible winter leaf colour in cultivars like 'Overture'.

Calamagrostis acutiflora *'Karl Foerster'*.

Calamagrostis (perennial)

C. × *acutiflora* is the feather reed grass from damp woodlands in Europe. Normally grown as the cultivar *C.* × *a.* 'Karl Foerster' for the mass of pinkish-bronze flower spikes that rise to head height, and startlingly upright in early summer. They turn that grassy biscuit colour later and stand well into winter. *C.* × *a.* 'Overdam' is smaller with variegated leaves, and *C. brachytricha* is more lax with feathery flower heads.

Calendula officinalis *'Indian Prince'*.

Calendula (hardy annual)

C. officinalis, the pot marigold, originates in the Mediterranean, but for centuries has been widely grown as both an ornamental and a herb. Relying largely for drought resistance on its long taproot, sowing direct into the ground is best. The daisy flowers, which occur over a long period through summer and autumn, are in the yellowy range and can be eaten. 'Fiesta Gitana' is a compact strain in a mix of soft yellows and orange. Its flowers are double and more pompom-like than the tall – to above your knees – 'Indian Prince'.

Catananche (biennial or perennial)

C. caerulea, also known as cupid's dart, is a daisy relative that grows in dry grassy places around the Mediterranean. It is actually a perennial, but short lived, and easily grown from seed, flowering well in the second year. From mid summer to autumn, dark eyed blue flowers are held to above knee height on wiry stems over a clump of grassy leaves. It will be more successfully perennial in really well drained soil. A taller Mediterranean relative, naturalized in northern Europe, is chicory, *Cichorium intybus*. It is similarly loose and natural looking, with blue flowers too.

Centaurea (hardy annual, perennial)
These are the knapweeds from dry mountain slopes and grassland in Europe, the Mediterranean region and eastwards. *C. nigra*, black knapweed, is a common perennial in wildflower seed mixes and an important wildlife plant. Its purple heads nestle amongst grasses in the summer meadow. For the garden border is *C. hypoleuca*, normally sold as *C. h.* 'John Coutts', with prettily divided soft green leaves and large heads of deep pink. It is low growing, to just above knee height, and spreads underground but not in a nasty way. These are all perennials, as is *C. Montana*, the perennial cornflower, a cottage garden favourite, growing to knee height but floppy, with its wispy flowers very early in summer. The actual cornflower, from cornfields of old, is the hardy annual *C. cyanus*, fairly tall, depending on the conditions, and slender, with cultivars to include white, pinks, reds and dark maroon.

Centaurea nigra.

Centaurea montana.

Centranthus ruber.

Cerinthe major *'Purpurascens'*.

Centranthus (perennial)
C. ruber is red valerian, from the Mediterranean, but widely naturalized on shingle beaches, old walls and other such inhospitable places. It sets seed freely in gardens, and is remarkably beautiful for a plant that many view as a weed. Seedlings are variable, with the fleshy leaves in different shades of green and flowers normally pink, but possibly white or red, appearing through summer to just above knee height. *Valeriana officinalis* (*see* page 38) is the closely related herb valerian. Native to much of Europe, it grows on dry hills but prefers moister grassland, where it will reach up to shoulder height, with pale pink flower clusters in early summer.

Cerinthe (hardy annual)
C. major is the Honeywort, an annual of dry grasslands in the Mediterranean region. It is nearly always grown as *C. major* 'Purpurascens', in which the flowers are purple, as opposed to yellow. They develop as drooping clusters at the tips of the stems, richly coloured but surrounded by leafy bracts of a softer purple that fades back down into the blue-green waxy foliage. It's an intriguing harmony of colour, on bushy plants, to above knee height, that most probably will pop up again next year from seed.

Cirsium (perennial)
C. rivulare is a spreading thistle of streamsides in central and southern Europe. Though that may sound like two reasons not to include it in a list of nice drought resistant plants, it has elegant poise and, in the cultivar *C. r.* 'Atropurpureum', deep crimson thistle heads. They appear from early to mid summer, up to waist height, but on dry sites you can expect them to be shorter.

Clarkia (hardy annual)
C. unguiculata, possibly sold as *C. elegans*, comes from dry rocky slopes in California. It's a cheery, flowery, easily grown annual, usually with double blooms to about knee height, in the lavender, pink, purple and red range. Alternatively, you could try *Clarkia amoena* (also known as *Godetia grandiflora*), of similar origin, but more available with single flowers to give it the natural look.

Convolvulus (hardy annual)
Convolvulus tricolor is an annual of dry open habitats around the Mediterranean. Its large, rich royal blue, funnel shaped flowers last for only one day, but are borne over a long period in summer. Naturally fairly small and bushy, to below knee height, the cultivar 'Blue Ensign' is selected for larger flowers on a more compact plant (*see* page 50).

Coreopsis (hardy annual, perennial)
C. verticillata is the thread-leaved tickseed, a North American perennial of woods and clearings on dry soils. Slender shoots below the ground extend slowly, giving rise each year to branching stems clothed with really finely divided foliage. Cheery star-like yellow daisies peer upwards and outwards

Coreopsis tinctoria.

from this frothy green cloud, and they can keep going all through summer. *C. v.* 'Moonbeam' has soft lemon-yellow flowers to knee height, but 'Zagreb' (*see* page 39) is shorter. *C. grandiflora* is another perennial tickseed from America, but it is often grown as a hardy annual in double flowered forms such as 'Sunray'. *Coreopsis tinctoria* is a true annual that brings a rich dark red colour into the range.

Coreopsis verticillata *'Moonbeam'*.

Coriandrum sativum.

Coriandrum sativum (annual)

C. sativum is the herb coriander, from dry grassy places around the Mediterranean. It grows quickly to about knee height, with finely divided aromatic edible foliage and frothy heads of tiny white flowers that produce the seeds used in flavouring. Sometimes called Chinese parsley it is closely related to *Petroselinum crispum*, the herb parsley, a biennial that is normally cut for the kitchen in its first year. Grown like this it needs a fair bit of moisture, but the curly-leaved form makes an attractive green foil in seasonal displays, where it doesn't need to be so lush and palatable.

Cosmos (hardy annual, half-hardy annual)

C. bipinnatus is a tap-rooted annual of dry open places like roadsides, in Mexico. With sturdy stems and very feathery leaves it can grow almost to head height, bearing, from mid-summer onwards, large yellow-centred daisies in pink, white and red. It is fine for sowing direct into the ground outdoors, in late spring, and will often reappear in subsequent years. Dwarf strains, such as Sonata Series, may be preferred in gardens. *C. sulphureus* is another Mexican annual, but with black centred flowers in the yellow-red range.

Cosmos bipinnatus.

Crambe cordifolia *with* Cynara scolymus.

Dianthus deltoides.

sturdy branched woolly grey stems to way above your head. These carry giant thistle-like flowers which open purple in summer and then stand dead as winter sculpture until wind and rain get the better of them. *C. scolymus*, the globe artichoke, is similar looking.

Crambe (perennial)

C. cordifolia is a deep rooted perennial from grassy and stony places in western Asia. Its large bold bristly leaves appear each year to form a deep green chunky mound, above which, in early summer, floats a billowing cloud of tiny white fragrant flowers. It's a big thing that needs a lot of space; you may need to look up at the flowers, particularly if it's in a fertile loamy soil. *C. maritima* is the sea kale (*see* page 143) of shingle beaches around Europe. Normally grown as a vegetable, the decorative value of its bold, waxy blue-green like foliage should not be overlooked, and the honey-scented, creamy coloured flowers will only come up to your knees.

Cynara

C. cardunculus, the cardoon, comes from dry grassland and stony places in southern Europe. Its leaves (*see* page 15) are enormous, deeply, divided and gracefully curved, forming large silvery clumps that punctuate the winter garden. Then in spring their volume expands threefold before pushing up

Dianthus (biennial and perennial)

The perennials include the plants we call pinks, derived mainly from wild European species of dry rocky hills. Most form shin high mounds of silvery blue, grass-like evergreen foliage, but it's the colours, shapes and scent of the flowers that they are grown for. In the old-fashioned cultivars, like the white and very frilly 'Mrs Sinkins', they appear for just a short period in early summer and are usually sweetly clove scented. This fragrance is found also in some of the repeat flowering modern pinks, like the white and purple 'Gran's favourite'. Alpine pinks have a simpler, more modest look, especially in natural species such as *D. deltoides*, the maiden pink, with white pink or red flowers over mats of dark green. *D. barbatus*, the Sweet William, grows on dry mountainsides in southern Europe. It has larger, greener, sometimes bronze-tinted leaves and is normally grown as a biennial. Low growing varieties are available and also taller ones up to knee height or more. They have flat clusters of sweetly scented flowers in all shades of red, pink and white, and many are bi-coloured. *Cerastium tomentosum*, or snow-in-summer, is a relative of pinks from mountain regions in Italy. It spreads vigorously, producing evergreen carpets of silvery foliage and little white flowers from late spring.

Dictamnus (perennial)

D. albus, or burning bush, is a deep rooted perennial of dry grassy, wooded or rocky places in southern Europe and many parts of Asia. Growing to just over knee height, it has attractive leathery leaves and upright spikes of elegant white flowers in early summer. *D. a.* var. *purpureus* will give prettily veined flowers of a soft mauve colour.

Digitalis lutea.

Dictamnus albus *var.* Purpureus.

Digitalis (biennial, perennial)

D. purpurea is the common foxglove (*see* page 32) of woodlands in western Europe. With spikes of trumpet shaped flowers, to head height, in early summer, they come in white as well as purple and pink in the wild, but commercial strains include colours like yellows and apricot. Common foxglove may sometimes survive beyond the first flowering, but there are species, such as *D. lutea*, that you can really depend on to be perennial.

Dipsacus (biennial)
D. fullonum is teasel from Europe, North Africa and Asia. It grows in all sorts of places, perhaps as a weed, but a wonderful plant nevertheless, both for wildlife and simple natural beauty. The flowering stem which develops from a withering rosette of pimply leaves is what holds the charm. It stands proud, to head height, and has leaves which clasp it in a way that holds water. You will see birds drinking from this, and in July the spiny egg-shaped heads of pinkish-purple flowers are a haven for bumblebees. Then the dead stem and flowers persist for months, as winter sculptures, providing seed for birds. And all of this, for no effort at all, once you've got it in the garden.

Dorotheanthus (hardy annual, half-hardy annual)
D. bellidiformis is the Livingstone daisy, from rocky and sandy places in South Africa. Its low mat of succulent, strangely glistening, leaves becomes completely covered in daisy-like flowers during mid-summer. Different shades of pinks, reds, orange yellow and white, often zoned within the same flower, create a stunning effect when in full flow on a sunny day. Suitable for sowing direct into warm soil, but with good drought resistance even when planted out in summer, it may be sold as *Mesembryanthemum criniflorum*. Other closely related South African succulents, for growing as annuals, are the equally low growing, reddish purple *Aptenia cordifolia* and the taller rose-pink *Lampranthus roseus*. They are actually perennials although not hardy. However, naturalized on the south-west coast of England is a close cousin to all of these – *Carpobrotus edulis*, the low sprawling decorative and edible Hottentot fig – which might be worth a try outside in the winter.

Dryopteris (perennial)
D. filix-mas is the male fern of woodlands and ditch banks in Europe, Asia and North America. One of a few good garden ferns for dry shade, this one is deciduous, forming feathery clumps to above knee height. *D. affinis* is similar but remains green through most of winter. *Polystichum setiferum*, the soft shield fern, is a true evergreen with fine lacy fronds, while the hart's tongue fern, *Asplenium scolopendrium*, is a smaller but boldly textured evergreen (*see* page 28).

Echinacea purpurea.

Echinacea (perennial)
E. purpurea, the coneflower, is one of the grand daisy plants of the North American prairies. From mid-summer through to autumn it has large reddish purple flower heads, each with a golden brown

centre. They stand proud on branching stems, possibly almost to shoulder height, but with neither particularly deep roots nor wilt-proof leaves, it will benefit from plenty of organic matter in the soil. *E. p.* 'Magnus' has particularly large and richly coloured flowers. Other cultivars offer whites, curious orangey colours and lower growth. Closely related is *Ratibida columnifera*, known as Mexican hat because of the upright 'cones' in the centre of the yellow daisies, which is better suited to really dry soil and flowers quickly from seed, so can be grown as an annual if required.

Echinops ritro *'Veitches Blue'*.

Echinops (perennial)

E. bannaticus and *E. ritro* are both species of globe thistle from dry rocky places in south-east Europe and thereabouts. They are similar to each other in general appearance, with perfectly spherical dense, steely-blue flower heads held aloft by statuesque stems, about waist height in late summer. The roots are deep and fleshy, and the leaves are elegantly shaped and slightly spiny: grey-green in *E. b.* 'Blue Globe' and darker in *E. r.* 'Veitches Blue'.

Echium (hardy annual, biennial)

E. vulgare is Viper's bugloss, from dry stony places and coastal cliffs in Europe. It grows to just over knee height, with rough hairy leaves and spikes of blue, sometimes pink or white, flowers in summer. The wild species is naturally biennial, but in certain, more compact cultivars, such as 'Blue Bedder', it performs well as a hardy annual. Something far more exotic for the south coast of England, or other warm spots where you dare to chance it, is *E. pininana*, a biennial from the Canary Islands. If it survives the winter, you should get a large vertical head of gigantic proportions the following summer. It grows up to twice the height of a tall man and is comprised of hundreds of blue flowers.

Eragrostis (perennial)

E. curvula is the weeping love grass from South Africa. It forms elegant evergreen mounds, to knee height, of really fine arching foliage and long airy flowering heads that also arch over. In *E. c.* 'Totnes Burgundy', the leaves turn a deep wine red as they mature.

Erigeron (perennial)

E. karvinskianus is from rocky places in Mexico and seeds itself freely in crevices around garden steps and walls. Little daisy flowers appear over delicate clumps of slender floppy stems all summer. They open white and then change to pink and purple, with all shades appearing on the plant at the same time. *E. glaucus* grows on sandy beaches in California, forming low evergreen mounds of grey-green leaves. For weeks on end, from late spring, it bears mauve yellow-centred daisies, more richly coloured in 'Sea Breeze'.

Erigeron glaucus 'Sea Breeze'.

Eryngium (perennial)

Most of the eryngiums that we grow in gardens occur in dry rocky mountain or coastal habitats in Europe, North Africa and Asia. From deep tap roots, and rosettes of lobed, or heart-shaped leaves, in summer they push up branched stems that bear dense rounded heads, each with its own leafy collar. Blues and whites predominate, and most species are fairly spiny. *E. maritimum*, the little sea holly of European sand dunes is a harmony of silvery blueness in leaf and flower. *E. giganteum* 'Silver Ghost' has a similar look, growing twice as tall, to above knee height. It is short lived but, if happy, will persist well through self-seeding. These really do need it dry, but other less silvery species are not so demanding. *E. bourgatii* has attractive white veined leaves and flowers at knee height. *E. planum* is a little taller. Also easily grown, though slightly less hardy, are the American species such as *E. agavifolium*. Their leaves are distinctively sword-shaped and flowers greenish white.

Eryngium bourgatii.

Erysimum linofolium *'Variegatum'*.

Eryngium agavifolium.

Erysimum (biennial, perennial)

E. cheiri is the wallflower, from southern Europe, where it grows on dry rocky slopes. A cottage garden favourite for centuries, and then the mainstay of spring bedding displays, it readily seeds into walls and paving. The yellow to red colour range is typical, as in the Bedder Series, but there are pinks and whites too, and most modern cultivars are compact, at well below knee height. *E. × allionii* is the Siberian wallflower, with very sweetly scented, brilliant orange flowers. These are both grown as biennials, but there are other wallflowers that do well when left in the ground from year to year. *E.* 'Bowle's Mauve' forms a shrubby base with evergreen leaves and upright heads of purple flowers over long periods from late winter. It grows to knee height, but *E. linifolium* 'Variegatum' is smaller.

Eschscholzia (hardy annual)

E. californica, the Californian poppy, is a fleshy rooted perennial of dunes and rocky hills. It is normally treated as a hardy annual, because flowering happens quickly from seed, and really good drainage is needed for winter survival. From a mat of finely divided hairy leaves, bright sunny weather will see the large orange poppy flowers open during late spring and summer. Usually about knee height in the natural species, most commercial seed strains are more compact, often with double flowers and with pinks and reds in the mix.

Eschscholzia californica.

Euphorbia characacias *subsp.* wulfenii.

Euphorbia (perennial)

Spurges grow in a wide range of habitats through-out the world, but frost-hardy species, with drought resistance, tend to occur in dry rocky hills and mead-ows in Europe and around the Mediterranean. The stems, which exude an irritant sap, generally per-sist through winter with leaves of a soft grey green colour, before the flower displays in greenish acid yellow appear in spring. *E. myrsinites* has succulent leaves and floppy stems that lie over the ground, while *E. cyparissias* forms spreading mats to shin height of feathery leaves. They are both bright and cheery in flower, but *E. characias* subsp. *wulfenii* is bigger, to shoulder height, with real visual punch. Lower growing woodland spurges with darker green leaves include the spreading ground cov-erer, *E. amygdaloides* var. *robbiae*, and the decidu-ous clump forming *E. polychroma*, which has really brightly coloured flowers for weeks.

Felicia (half-hardy annual)

F. bergeriana, the Kingfisher daisy, is from dry open soils in South Africa. It forms a low mat of grey-green, slightly hairy leaves, and then for long peri-ods in summer it produces yellow-centred daisies with slender rays of brilliant electric blue. Another low growing blue daisy, for bedding out, is the Aus-tralian Swan River daisy, *Brachyscome iberidifolia*. It has feathery foliage and comes in pinks, whites and purples as well.

Foeniculum vulgare.

Foeniculum (perennial)

F. vulgare is the herb fennel. Growing wild on stony ground round the north coast of the Mediterranean, it is a beautiful delicate plant from the first unfurling of the threadlike leaves in spring. The cloud of foliage that develops gives rise in summer to flat heads of yellowish green flowers which stand dead at eye level, in a sculptural kind of way, for some time while they seed around. *F. v.* 'Purpureum', with soft warming bronze foliage, is the one normally grown for ornament (*see* page 28). There is a giant fennel too, *Ferula communis*. Its leaves are not quite so feathery, but shiny and lacy, and the enormous yellow flowering, which takes a few years to happen, will often be the last thing it does.

Gaillardia (hardy annual, perennial)

This is a group of daisies from dry American prairie grassland. They are normally grown as *Gaillardia × grandiflora*, a hybrid between a perennial and an annual species. Many of the cultivars can be either sown direct and discarded in autumn, or kept in the ground as short-lived perennials. They have slightly floppy stems, soft green leaves and large dazzling daisy flowers all through summer. The most striking of all combine two hot colours, as in the low growing 'Kobold'; rich red surrounded with fiery yellow.

Gaura (perennial)

G. lindheimeri is a deep rooted perennial of hot dry locations in the American prairies. For something loose, shaggy and pretty, you need look no further. It forms a big willowy clump, to shoulder height, of slender leaved stems, spangled with little pinkish white flowers from May through to autumn. Flowering from seed in the first year, it can be treated as an annual if your winters are too cold and wet. The cultivar 'Siskiyou Pink' is more compact and richer toned in its flowers and foliage.

Gazania (half-hardy annual)

These brightly coloured African daisies from sandy plains and mountain slopes are really only grown in gardens as hybrid cultivars. Although evergreen perennials that take a touch of frost, they are most easily treated as annuals for summer bedding. With handsome leaves, usually waxy on top and felted beneath, they remain fairly independent after summer planting, and given sunny days will show off their big smiley daisies well into autumn. All have foliage fairly close to the ground with flowers looking up from just above. Whites, pinks, yellows, oranges and bronze shades predominate, so you may want to be sensible and go for a single colour.

Geranium (perennial)

As distinct from pelargonium (*see* page 116), these are the hardy cranesbills that occur across the globe in habitats such as dry woodlands, grasslands and rocky hillsides. They are easy both to grow and to look at, pretty in foliage and flower, with a modest natural look that just seems to blend in. A number of European species are particularly useful. *G. sanguineum* var. *striatum* is a form of the bloody cranesbill, with soft pink summer flowers on low spreading mats of finely textured foliage. It's one for sunny spots, whereas the evergreen *G. macrorrhizum* 'Ingwersen's Variety' does well in shade, with pale pink flowers in late spring and chunkier, aromatic foliage that turns to red tints in autumn. If an old garden has been completely taken over with pink evergreen knee-high geranium, it's likely to be *G. endressii*, just showing how easily pleased it is, flowering for weeks through summer. Blues are

Gaura lindheimeri.

Geranium pratense.

important too, not least in the meadow cranesbill, *G. pratense*, which does well in long rough grassland. It is relatively tall, to above knee height, as is the rich magenta flowered *G. psilostemon* (*see* page 120) from north-east Turkey. From the Caucasus mountains nearby comes *G. renardii*, with white flowers over little mounds of grey-green velvety foliage. Other smaller alpines belong to the related genus *Erodium*.

Gypsophila (hardy annual, perennial)
G. paniculata, or baby's breath, is a deep rooted perennial of dry sandy grassland and stony ground in eastern Europe through to Siberia. Each spring, it forms a broad mound of twiggy branching stems, clothed sparsely with slender leaves. Mid-summer sees this enlivened by a haze of tiny white flowers, forming a cloud to waist height or more. *G.* 'Rosen-

schleier' has a similar effect but is lower and spreading, with double flowers that open white, then turn pale pink. Annual baby's breath, *G. elegans*, grows upright to a similar height and is available in seed strains from white through to the deeper shades of pink.

Gypsophila paniculata.

Helianthus *'Lemon Queen'*.

Helianthus (hardy annual, perennial)
This all-American genus includes the sunflower, *H. annuus* (*see* page 79), of dry, and sometimes not so dry, open plains in the West. Famously tall, with those massive daisies, many seed strains now are of more moderate proportions with branching stems bearing a number of heads. 'Autumn Beauty' embraces the full colour range, from deep earthy reds to lemon yellow, at a height just below eye level. 'Russian Giant' is a good old-fashioned big sunflower, and with the large central disc, gives plenty of seeds for eating. The Jerusalem artichoke (*H. tuberosus*), grown for its edible tubers, is a par-

ent of the popular perennial garden hybrid, *H.* 'Lemon Queen', a really easily grown perennial, to head height, with soft yellow daisies for weeks from late summer.

Helictotrichon (perennial)
H. sempervirens, or blue oat grass, forms dense tufted evergreen mounds on dry hillsides in south-west Europe. With soft grey-blue foliage to knee height, and silvery flower heads that mature to a warm straw colour, it's a perfect ornamental grass for the dry garden.

Helictotrichon
sempervirens.

Hemerocallis 'Stafford'.

Hemerocallis (perennial)

Day lilies come from the Far East, where they grow in open woods and grassland, often on quite wet soils. From a large fleshy underground stem, they produce elegant arching leaves, grassy though sometimes quite broad, and of a fresh lively green in spring. Slender stalks emerge during summer, bearing lily-like flowers, mainly in yellows, orange and red. While they only last a day, more open tomorrow, and modern American breeding has given rise to longer lasting flowers, appearing over longer periods, in all sorts of colours, on compact plants – the list of cultivars is endless. But it's the wilder species and older, less hybridized varieties, in the original colours, that are likely to be most self-reliant. *H. lilioasphodelus* bears fragrant yellow flowers early in the season, and *H. fulva* 'Europa', tawny orange flowers later on; both are vigorous spreading plants to above knee height with tasty flowers. Good, tried and tested, free-flowering hybrids include the mahogany red 'Stafford' and lemon yellow 'Hyperion'.

Iberis (hardy annual, perennial)

The candytufts come from coastal cliffs and rocky hills around the Mediterranean. *I. umbellata* is the common annual species, with bobble heads of fragrant flowers in white, pinks, purples and bright reds. Below knee height, or a good deal lower, fine colour blends such as 'Flash Mixed' flower over long periods and could hardly be easier to grow. *I. sempervirens* is a low spreading evergreen perennial of the same ilk as Arabis and Aubrieta (*see* page 86) but with dark green foliage and those bobble heads.

Iris (perennial)

There are all sorts of irises growing in all sorts of places all through the Northern Hemisphere. Even amongst those from dry habitats, there are many very different types. The bearded irises range from ankle to hip height, with broad sword-like leaves

Iberis sempervirens.

Iris pallida.

is the season also of the little bulbous *I. reticulata*, with purplish flowers just above the ground. Moving away from the dry and sunny, there is *I. sibirica*, from wetlands in Europe and Russia. It is remarkably unfussy, with elegant flowers, in blues, purples, pink and white, up to hip height, in early summer. Then, for the woodland garden, is the European evergreen *I. foetidissima*, grown for its winter clusters of bright orangey-red seeds.

Kniphofia (perennial)

Most red hot pokers occur naturally on streamsides and damp ground in South Africa, but cope well with dry conditions too. From thick fleshy underground parts, they produce tussocks of grassy foliage and solid upright flower spikes in spring, summer or autumn. The dazzling colour combinations demand attention, and their unwavering rigidity is a welcome contrast to looser plants such as grasses. *K. uvaria* and *K. linearifolia* are classic

arising from stout rhizomes and extravagant blooms of various colours in early summer. One species from which they originate is *I. pallida* from rocky hillsides in eastern Europe. It has grey-green leaves, soft blue flowers, and there are a couple of really good variegated forms. *I. ungicularis* has no hairy bits on the petals, so is beardless. From hot rocky places, south and east of the Mediterranean, its blue flowers appear amongst knee high tufts of grassy evergreen foliage in winter and spring. This

Kniphofia linearifolia.

Kniphofia *'Strawberries and Cream'*.

hot pokers with flowers around shoulder height, fading through orange and yellow. They form large clumps of fairly chunky evergreen leaves and flower in autumn. *K.* 'Atlanta' is similar but spring flowering. Many of the newer garden cultivars, with less traditional colours, are smaller, with finer deciduous foliage and flowers appearing in summer.

Lathyrus (perennial)
L. latifolius is the everlasting pea, native to much of Europe and naturalized elsewhere amongst shrubs and hedges. It is one of a small number of herbaceous perennial climbers that we grow in gardens, reaching head height or more by clambering over other plants or any wiry support you might give it. From a tangle of curiously winged stems and blue-green leaves, it bears clusters of large pink or purple flowers over a long period through late summer.

Lavatera (hardy annual)
L. trimestris is a tall, elegant, tap-rooted annual from sandy coastal places around the Mediterranean. It has broad funnel-shaped flowers through summer, in white or shades of pink, to above knee

Lathyrus latifolius.

Lavatera trimestris *'Silver Cup'*.

height. The petals are often attractively veined, as in the rose-pink 'Silver Cup' (*see* also the shrubby lavateras on page . . .).

Leymus (perennial)

L. arenarius is a rapidly spreading grass that stabilizes coastal dunes in Europe. It has arching leaves, bluish in colour, and wheat-like flower heads to shoulder height in summer. *Elymus magellanicus*, from South America, is another grass; much smaller, more evergreen and less invasive, it's planted for the intensely blue colour of its leaves (*see* page 36).

Limonium (half-hardy annual, perennial)

L. latifolium is a perennial from dry grassland in south-east Europe. From its tough searching root system, a rosette of long leathery evergreen leaves gives rise in late summer to the flowering stems. Reaching knee height, they branch in all directions to form a cloud of deep lavender blue that lasts for weeks. The Mediterranean coastal species, *L. sinuatum*, is the florist's statice. Actually a perennial, but best as a half-hardy annual, you could, in warmer gardens, sow it direct. The stiffly branched

stems, to knee height, are curiously winged and, in selected cultivars, bear small papery flowers in almost every imaginable colour. *Phyllostachys suworowii*, a close relative from central Asia, is a half-hardy annual, to about the same height, with long branching spikes of tiny pink flowers.

Linaria (perennial)

These plants, known as toadflax, come mainly from cliffs, rocky slopes and dry grassland in Europe and around the Mediterranean. The purple toadflax, *Linaria purpurea*, is widely naturalized, often appearing as seedlings in gardens. Sturdy, upright stems bearing grey-green leaves, grow up to waist height where they are topped with long vertical spikes of tiny purple flowers. It is slender, graceful and flowers all through summer, so you would have to be a real stickler for tidiness to weed it out. If you need to buy one, then try the softer coloured *L. p.* 'Canon Went'. Common toadflax, *L. vulgaris*, is one for the wild garden. It is generally shorter than purple toadflax with heads of pale yellow flowers. The modest but cheery toadflax character appears also in the hardy annual *L. maroccana* and its colour mixed strains.

Phsyllostachys suworowii.

Linaria maroccana *'Fairy Bouquet'*.

Linaria purpurea *'Canon J. Went'*.

Linum perenne.

Linum (hardy annual, perennial)
The flaxes are fine airy plants with slender leaves and stems. *L. perenne* grows on dry grassy hills in Europe through to central Asia. It is fairly short lived but survives a few seasons given adequate drainage, and each day during early-mid summer produces a fresh crop of clear blue flowers at about knee height. Of similar stature is *L. grandiflorum* from North Africa, an annual for direct sowing. It is probably best as *L. g.* 'Rubrum', with flowers, in summer, of the warmest crimson red.

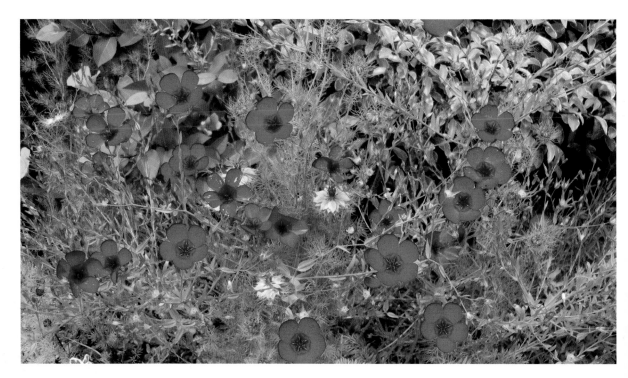

Linum grandiflorum *'Rubrum'*.

Liriope (perennial)
L. muscari, or lilyturf, is a low growing evergreen perennial from woodland floors in the Far East. It forms dense, slowly spreading clumps of tough evergreen grassy leaves, with solid spikes of bright mauve flowers in autumn. *L. m.* 'Variegata' is good for foliage, and in 'Monroe White' the flowers show well against deep green leaves. *Ophiopogon*, also known as lilyturf, is a closely related genus with similar origins. Popular for its mat of black foliage is *O. planiscapus* 'Nigrescens', while the very low growing *O. japonicus* 'Minor' has fine grassy leaves that can make a turf-like surface in shade.

Lobularia (hardy annual)
L. maritima is sweet alyssum, from dry sunny places around the Mediterranean. It is often treated as a half-hardy annual and planted in summer bedding or containers, for its thousands of tiny, sweetly scented flowers. There are many good cultivars, all easy to grow, about ankle high and with long flowering periods. 'Carpet of Snow' is the typical white, but there are pink and deep purple ones too.

Liriope muscari.

Lunaria (biennial)

L. annua is a biennial species of fairly moist, usually shady, places in south-east Europe. We call it honesty, and it's true to say that it has almost all we could wish for in a plant: pretty spring flowers that attract butterflies, translucent spherical seed heads which decorate the house or feed the birds, and big lush heart shaped leaves. It self-seeds, but not uncontrollably, so maintains well-behaved garden populations that do not need watering. Purple is the normal colour, but there is a white one too, and strikingly variegated forms of each.

Lychnis (perennial)

Lychnis coronaria, or dusty miller, grows in dry shrubland and on rocky slopes in south-east Europe. It is a hairy leaved perennial, though short-lived, and often self-seeds to form waist height clumps of silvery leaves that make a fitting backdrop for the purple flowers. These are borne over several weeks from early summer, harmonizing well with the foliage in the white form *L. c.* 'Alba'. *L. × walkeri* 'Abbotswood Rose' makes a broad clump, only to knee height, of the same coloured leaves but with flowers of rich piercing pink.

Lychnis × walkeri *'Abbotswood Rose'.*

Malva moschata.

Malva (perennial)

M. moschata, the musk mallow, is native to most of Europe, growing in dry grassy places, quite often on roadsides. From a strong branching taproot, it produces a bushy clump of prettily divided leaves, to well above knee height. The flowers, pale pink, or white in *M. m.* f. *alba*, appear all through summer. Short-lived as a perennial, it is sometimes grown as a biennial and self-seeds where sunny and dry enough.

Matthiola (hardy annual, biennial)

M. incana, the hoary stock or gillyflower, occurs naturally on exposed coastal sites in the Mediterranean. It has grey hairy leaves and upright heads of sweetly scented flowers. Brompton stock is the traditional strain for biennial cultivation, and it is normally sold as 'Brompton Lady' in a mix of colours from strong reds through lavender to white. Plants come up to knee height, with fragrant flowers appearing in late spring – some double, some single – in solid vertical heads. Other strains, such as the very quick to flower 'Ten Week Mixed', are grown as annuals.

Mentzelia (hardy annual)

M. lindleyi, or Blazing Star, comes from open rocky slopes in California. You may find the seed sold as *Bartonia aurea*. It can grow quite tall, to knee height, and straggly, but has a casual natural look, mingling well with other plants. In a long hot summer, it will keep producing large star shaped, bright golden yellow flowers that open in late afternoon to give evening fragrance.

Miscanthus (perennial)

M. sinensis is a tall deciduous meadow grass from the Far East. From a bulky clump of lush foliage it pushes up flowering stems in autumn to way above head height. Like clusters of long feathery fingers, silvery grey with a hint of purple, they stand dead all through winter with a pale biscuit colour (*see* page 79). An extraordinary plant with many cultivars of different heights, some arching, some upright, and some with strong reddish tints in the flowers.

Miscanthus sinensis *'Ferner Osten'*.

Myosotis (biennial)

M. sylvatica is a wild forget-me-not of European woods, hedge banks and grassland. It is the species from which many cultivars have been developed. Adding pinks and whites to the natural blue, in a long flowering season, on compact plants, these are a common component of spring bedding schemes. They self-seed readily, so gardens often have a wild population which seems able to pop up almost anywhere.

Nepeta (perennial)

Plants in this genus come from dry rocky places in Europe, North Africa and Asia. Most frequently seen is the catmint, *N. × faassenii*. It forms spreading clumps of grey-green aromatic foliage, with sprays of lavender blue flowers to knee height, that can go on right through summer. *N.* 'Walkers Low' is a fair bit taller actually, but with good tidy growth and a profuse display of richly coloured flowers.

Nerine (perennial)

N. bowdenii is an autumn flowering South African bulb from hot dry rocky and stony places. The strap-shaped leaves appear in summer, then disappear before the display of flowers, rich pink normally but white in the form *alba*.

Nerine bowdenii.

Nigella (hardy annual)

N. damascena, or Love-in-a-mist, is a very short lived annual from all sorts of dry sunny places around the Mediterranean. In gardens it self-sows, from inflated seed capsules, and usually gives a second generation each year. From a tough tap-root, the stem bears really fine lacy foliage, some of which grows like a big feathery collar, around each flower. Self-sown, they tend to be pale blue and single, but commercial seed strains provide fuller flowers in darker blue, pink and white.

Oenothera (biennial, perennial)

The evening primroses are from southern US and Mexico, growing in sandy or rocky places. The familiar one is *O. biennis*, a useful food plant that's widely naturalized and often seen as a garden weed. Pretty it is too, in a wild kind of way, with soft yellow perfumed flowers that open on summer evenings, to the great delight of night flying moths. They fade the next day, but there are plenty more, so flowering continues for weeks into autumn. Its tall biennial growth, to head height, is in stark contrast to the low, sprawling perennial, *O. macrocarpa*. With blooms, perhaps as big as your hand, in bright yellow, it grows from a single deep root so cannot become invasive, while the white fragrant flowered *O. speciosa* spreads underground and possibly can. But they both have daytime flowers through the full length of summer, and in *O. s.* 'Siskiyou', they are of a soft delicate pink.

Onopordum (biennial)

O. acanthium is the cotton thistle that occurs throughout Europe on bare and cultivated ground. It is a true biennial, producing large spiny basal leaves, coated in silvery hairs (*see* page 80). In the second year they expand to form an enormous rosette from which the flower stems arise. Also spiny and silver, these can reach way up above head height and bear purple, or sometimes white, thistle-like heads. It's the sheer, bold architectural presence of the plant that is important though, surely the grandest weed in the garden, when it comes to thinning out its seedlings.

Onopordum acanthium.

Origanum (perennial)

O. vulgare is wild marjoram, the herb of dry grasslands throughout Europe and much of Asia. It can vary in size and shape, and the loose heads of summer flowers may be white or pink. But richly aromatic foliage there will always be, sometimes golden or variegated in selected cultivars. *O. laevigatum* 'Herrenhausen' has a purple tinge in winter and dense heads of pink flowers. At knee height it is much taller than *O.* 'Kent Beauty' which has large pink bracts with its flowers.

Origanum *'Kent Beauty'*.

Osteospermum jucundum.

Osteospermum (half-hardy annual, perennial)
O. jucundum comes from South Africa, where it grows in fairly moist grassy and rocky places. From a spreading evergreen carpet of grey-green leaves it can send up flowering stems continuously between late spring and autumn. At about knee height, they each bare a single, elegant purplish pink daisy. Most other osteospermums are only marginally hardy at best, though they do make good summer bedding plants, and some, such as *O. ecklonis* 'Ballade Mixed', can be grown from seed. Another South African, closely related, is *Dimorphotheca sinuata*, the Star of the Veldt. A genuine annual, its pastel mixes of white, yellows, orange and pink can be obtained from direct sowing into warm ground.

Papaver (hardy annual, perennial)
P. orientale is a poppy from meadows and stony mountain slopes in western Asia. Typical of the genus, with fleshy roots, hairy leaves, promising buds, and pepper-pot seed heads, its big colourful papery flowers appear from late spring to mid summer. That's when the leaves die back, but it is a reliable perennial, and it comes in a wide range of cultivars; all of about knee height or more, they're not all the classic scarlet and black. The annuals are weeds of cultivated ground but still have those flowers. From the common field poppy, *Papaver*

Papaver rhoeas.

rhoeas, comes Shirley Series – reds, pinks, orange and yellow, prettily blended with white. Some of these are double, a feature taken to the extreme in the frilly and pink opium poppy, *Papaver somniferum* 'Paeony Flowered'.

Pelargonium (half-hardy annual)
These are the non-hardy geraniums used in summer bedding and containers. The zonal pelargoniums, derived from wild plants of dry rocky hills in South Africa, are the most commonly grown. They have succulent stems, and rounded leaves, often distinctively marked, but it is the flowers we normally grow them for. There are hundreds of cultivars, most of which would have to be bought as plants. But seed strains, such as those in the long flowering Multibloom Series, can be treated as annuals, as can the 'Summer Showers' mix of the trailing, ivy-leaved varieties. Pelargonium colours range from red through all sorts of pinks, purples and mauve, to white. They are actually perennials if you overwinter them carefully, which you may well want to try, once you know the cost of buying more seed.

Pennisetum (annual, perennial)
P. alopecuroides is the clump-forming fountain grass from the Far East and western Australia.

Most commonly grown as *P. a.* 'Hameln', it grows to knee height with soft whitish bottlebrush-like flower heads that become grey-brown on maturing in late summer. *P. setaceum* is best treated as an annual, for the rich colouration of its leaves and flowers when grown in forms such as 'Rubrum'.

Penstemon 'Evelyn'.

Penstemon (perennial)
This is a large genus of plants from Central and North America, grown for their long lasting displays of colourful trumpet shaped flowers. They occur wild in a variety of habitats, but it's the slightly shrubby mountain species that cope best with frost and drought. These include *P. pinifolius* and its cultivar 'Wisley Flame', low growing at shin height, with really fine needle-like leaves and slender orangey-red flowers in summer. Another is the stronger growing and coarser leaved *P. heterophyllus*, which in the cultivar 'Heavenly Blue' grows to about knee height with blue flowers tinged purple. Most of the popular hybrids are completely non-woody and not always so hardy. One of the toughest is 'Evelyn', relatively small, at just over knee height, with fine textured foliage and flowers from mid-summer onwards.

Phormium (perennial)
P. tenax, the New Zealand flax, is actually a species of wet fields and swamps, but it adapts well to drier conditions and looks at home amongst gravel and stones. Its bold, leathery strap-like leaves form gigantic evergreen clumps, but most garden cultivars are smaller, derived from crosses with the less bulky mountain flax, *P. cookianum*. Another New Zealander, this species of coastal cliffs and rocky places has leaves less rigid, and the tubular flowers that rise up through them are yellowy, as opposed to dullish red in *P. tenax*. But it's the foliage we grow them for, and with the stripes on the leaves of the hybrids, it seems there is every colour except blue. In colder wetter gardens, cultivars of *P. tenax* such as the 'Purpureum' or 'Variegata' would do best, but elsewhere you have the full choice of colours and sizes. 'Yellow Wave' and 'Platt's Black' (*see* page 71), from opposite ends of the light-dark spectrum, are just over knee height with arching foliage.

Phuopsis (perennial)
P. stylosa is a low-spreading perennial, originally from open woodland and hillsides in parts of Western Asia. It has attractively textured foliage and rounded heads of little pink flowers through summer. A close relative from Europe is *Galium verum*, or lady's bedstraw, which produces a frothy display of bright yellow in summer meadows (*see* page 132).

Portulaca (half-hardy annual)
P. grandiflora is a low sprawling plant of dry sandy soils in South America. Grown as an annual for bedding out in summer, its plight is aided by having slender, fleshy succulent leaves. The flowers in commercial seed strains are normally double in many bright shades of yellow and red.

Salvia coccinea *'Lady in Red'*.

Salvia (hardy annual, half-hardy annual, biennial, perennial)
S. nemorosa is a hardy herbaceous cousin of the herb sage (*see* page 74), from dry meadows and rocky hills in parts of Europe and western Asia, grown for its summer display of strong dense upright blue heads – they reach knee height in *S. n.* 'Ostfriesland', but are taller in the related hybrid, *S. × superba*. Similar to these in homeland and habitat is the biennial kitchen herb clary, *S. sclarea* (*see* page 140). From its large coarse overwintering foliage grow enormous branched flower heads of pink and white

Salvia nemorosa
'Ostfriesland'.

in early summer. *S. horminum*, from the Mediterranean, is the hardy annual clary with flowers, at knee height, of pink, blue, purple or white. From the same region comes the biennial *S. argentea*. Less conspicuous in flower, this is grown mainly for its large, really silvery leaves. *S. coccinea*, scarlet sage, and *S. farinacea*, the mealy sage, are two American species grown as half-hardy annuals. *S. c.* 'Lady in Red' and *S. f.* 'Victoria' (*see* page 80), with spikes of deepest blue, each produce upright spikes that grow taller than most summer bedding, and give lots of colour right through to autumn.

Sedum (perennial)

S. spectabile, the ice plant, is a species of rocky cliffs, and sometimes moister places, in the Far East. Its

stems grow to knee height, bearing fleshy grey-green leaves and large flat heads of pink flowers in late summer. *S. telephium* subsp. *maximum*, from Europe and eastern Asia, is similar but less attractive in flower, though often grown as 'Atropurpureum' with stems and leaves of rich dark purple. There are low trailing ones too, with late summer flowers such as *S.* 'Ruby Glow'. These are all truly herbaceous, from relatively hospitable habitats, but other sedums, or stonecrops, are very low growing succulent evergreens from extremely dry, exposed, often coastal locations. They include the European *S. acre* with yellow flowers, and the American *S. spathulifolium*, grown for coloured foliage.

Sempervivum (perennial)

The houseleeks are mat-forming evergreen succulents from rocky mountainous parts of Europe and Asia. Their tightly packed rosettes are replaced anew after the summer flower display (*see* page 16). Dozens of cultivars there are, all very collectable.

Silybum (biennial)

S. marianum is the milk thistle from the Mediterranean region and west Asia, where it grows mainly on

Sedum spectabile *'Brilliant'*.

Silybum marianum.

roadsides and field margins. The large flat rosette of thistly leaves, with their boldly marked white veins, is the main reason to grow it, but the purple thistle heads are worthy of admiration too, reaching up to shoulder height, rose-purple and sweetly scented; there are some gardeners who cut them off for the sake of prolonging the foliage display. It is one of the very few plants that are naturally variegated, and what's more, it's nearly all edible.

Stachys (perennial)

S. byzantina is the very woolly leaved plant called lamb's ears. From rocky hills in western Asia, it produces a mat of foliage, and vertical stems, to knee height or more, throughout summer. The little pinkish flowers they bear are rather outshone by the white wooliness around them, and some gardeners prefer *S. b.* 'Silver Carpet' for its especially good foliage and failure to flower.

Stachys byzantina.

Stipa tenuissima *with* Geranium psilostemon.

Stipa (perennial)
S. gigantea, the giant feather grass, is a clump-forming evergreen from dry rocky slopes in the Mediterranean region. Grown for its large open flower heads, to above head height, they are most spectacular on maturing to a warm golden glow in late summer. The New Zealander, *S. arundinacea*, forms a waist high mound of orangey-brown tinted leaves with a frothy coating of golden flowers from late summer. Then, of similar height, from Central and South America, is *S. tenuissima*, with upright tufts of really slender hair-like leaves that constantly fidget in the breeze.

Tagetes (hardy, half-hardy annual)
Much maligned amongst gardeners now for their brash, oversized flowers, it is probably the African marigolds (derived from *T. erecta*) that would mostly boast those qualities. Cultivars of *T. patula*, the French marigold from dry slopes in Central

America, are smaller in all parts, sometimes with single flowers. Brash yellows and oranges they are though, all through summer, sometimes combined with deep red as in 'Naughty Marietta'. The foliage, to shin height, is prettily divided and aromatic, arising from a tap-root, which will be most effective if direct sown in late spring. This also suits well the more elegant, single flowered, Signet marigolds, derived from *T. tenuifolia*.

Thymus (perennial)
The thymes are low perennials or small shrubby plants of dry grassland and sandy places, mainly in Europe and western Asia. *T. vulgaris* (garden thyme) and *T. × citriodorus* (lemon thyme) are often used as herbs, but there are decorative coloured leaved forms of each. They are both quite bushy with slender woody stems, unlike creeping species such as *T. serpyllum* and the woolly leaved *T. pseudolanuginosus*.

Thymus pseudolanuginosus.

Tulipa (biennial, perennial)

An enormous group of bulbous perennials, they are mainly from dry habitats in central Asia. Some, such as the Darwin Hybrid and Triumph groups, are used in spring bedding schemes so, in that sense, are treated as biennials. Others, notably the Kaufmanniana and Greigii groups of cultivars, can be grown as perennials if kept free from waterlogging in winter. They are small plants with an early display of large, often multiple coloured, cup-shaped flowers.

Verbascum (biennial, perennial)

The mulleins come mainly from Europe and Asia, where they grow in various dry, sparsely vegetated, and exposed places. *V. thapsus*, the great mullein, is widely distributed, and good for the wild garden. Typical of the genus, it has soft silver woolly leaves

Verbascum chaixii f. album.

Verbena rigida.

and a tall upright stem bearing many small saucer shaped yellow flowers over summer. The Greek species *V. olympicum* is similar, but usually larger, to head height or above, and more flowery. At half that height is the perennial *V. chaixii,* often grown in the white form with mauve centres to its flowers. This departure from the normal yellow is complete in *V. phoeniceum.* A perennial with dark green leaves, and flowers varying from white through pink to purple, it has been used in breeding to produce good perennial cultivars, such as those listed under the Cotswold group.

Verbena (half-hardy annual, perennial)
These are mainly from grassy or rocky ground in America and include cultivars under the name *V.* × *hybrida* that are grown for summer bedding and hanging baskets. Although reasonably drought resistant, it is the hardier perennials that give most value in dry summers. *V. bonariensis* can reach head height with long slender, almost leafless stems, holding up the heads of purple flowers for weeks through late summer. It seeds itself freely, appearing here and there without interfering with other plants. Similar in flower is *V. rigida,* knee height and spreading below ground where happy. The more feathery leaves of *V. tenera* are seen in gardens on hybrids such as the mat forming *V.* 'Sissinghurst', with bright pink flowers from May until the frosts. All South American, these are not as hardy as *V. canadensis* and its cultivar 'Homestead Purple', also low and spreading and flowering for months.

Vinca (perennial)
V. major and *V. minor* are the greater and lesser periwinkles, from woods and hedgerows in Europe. They are vigorous evergreens, with rooting stems that form ever-spreading ground cover. The knee-high tangle of *V. major* is not what is usually required in home gardens, but its lesser cousin is better behaved, forming a dense low mat, with pretty blue flowers from April to June. 'Gertrude Jekyll' is particularly compact with white flowers.

Zinnia (hardy, half-hardy annual)

Z. elegans is a purple daisy from dry open habitat in Mexico. It has quite broad, slightly hairy leaves, and in the wild form can grow up well above knee height. Garden seed strains come in the full colour range, almost anything except blue. They show different degrees of compactness, and usually have double flowers. Further variety is available from *Z. haageana*, such as in the compact 'Aztec Sunset', and though they are all often treated as half-hardy annuals, sowing direct outside late in spring is fine. Also from Mexico, but hardier still, is the plant called creeping zinnia, *Sanvitalia procumbens*. It is suitable for outdoor sowing in early spring, or even autumn, when it will flower all through the following summer.

LEFT: Zinnia haageana *'Aztec Sunset'*.

BELOW: Sanvitalia procumbens.

CHAPTER 4

Planting and garden care

PLANTING

Not to deny the importance of paving and walls that need to be built before you can plant – they make the garden usable, in the way that you want, and go a long way towards giving it style. But it's the plants that really bring life to a garden, as long as there is water, of course. Bringing them in, and getting them growing, is where we succeed, or not, in our efforts to be wise with that water.

The more you want plants to grow really well, as in a vegetable plot, or a lush flowery border, the more water they will need. The fussier they are, and the less your soil is suited to them, the greater will be the need to alter it. Clearing weeds and improving soil structure, to make water more available, are key elements in preparing ground for planting. Altering pH, increasing nutrient levels and improving drainage, may also be important.

Preparing the ground

The best chance you will ever have to get rid of weeds is before you plant. In fact, before you dig, or do anything, is the time to see what types of weed you've got.

There are annual weeds like chickweed and groundsel, and perennial ones like nettles, bindweed and dock. Many of the annuals are actually ephemerals, going through several generations in only one year. This is their strength and why they are such clever weeds. They will germinate, flower and seed in no time at all, especially in hot dry conditions, and if allowed to do this you will get more and more of them again and again, whenever you turn the soil. The way to control them is regular hoeing, so they don't even get to think about flow-

ering. Done early on a hot dry day, you can leave them there to shrivel in the sun.

Perennial weeds take hold most easily amongst permanent plantings that are not regularly dug over. They get their roots down and spread themselves out, competing vigorously for light, nutrients and water. Pieces of root or rhizome that remain in the ground after weeding will grow back with a vengeance, so you need to be thorough with the border fork or herbicide. Easier said than done – they can romp away in summer and get entwined with the roots of your plants, deeming them not even worthy of the compost heap. Dock and dandelion don't do this, but they seed like annuals and grow back up from any little bits of taproot that get left in the ground.

If your weeds are the difficult perennial ones, a weed killer might be the best option. Weed killers containing glyphosate work best in this situation, applied when the weeds are actively growing and leafy enough to absorb the chemical. Smothering them with a membrane is another option, if you can wait a couple of years, and if not, you can plant through the membrane so it becomes a kind of mulch. But it won't let you garden any more on that piece of ground, and if there are lots of weeds, they will come up through the holes. The only other alternative, after a deep sigh, is the committed determination to dig every little bit out, and then to see that through. Depending on the weeds and the soil, it may be possible, but not just in one digging, so you will need to go back again and again.

Annual weeds are less of an issue when preparing the ground. You should chop them down or dig them in to stop them seeding, but there are probably lots of seeds in the ground that will come up

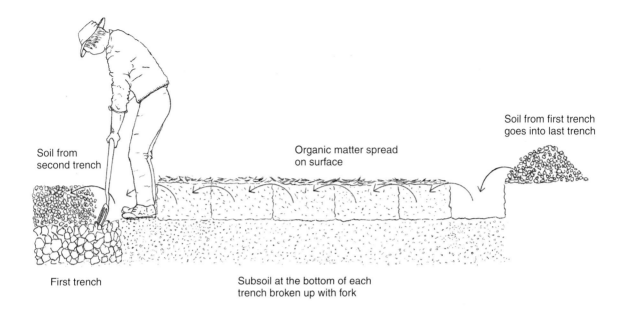

Soil from first trench goes into last trench

Organic matter spread on surface

Soil from second trench

First trench

Subsoil at the bottom of each trench broken up with fork

Double-digging.

as soon as you dig. The other option therefore is the no-dig method.

A major reason for digging over ground before planting or sowing is to break up compaction or soil pans that will restrict root growth and drainage. If there is no problem with soil structure down to two spade depths, there may well be no benefit from digging. The no-dig approach is often used in vegetable gardening, where the crops are grown on small beds that are not trodden on (*see* page 138), and it could also be used in preparing ground for permanent planting. Shrubs respond well, provided the soil suits them; each one is planted into its own little pit and then the whole bed mulched over the top.

The benefits of not digging are:
- Less growth of annual weeds because you don't bring lots of seeds to the surface;
- Less compaction caused by standing on the ground;
- Worms are left undisturbed, but they will need lots of organic matter laid on top;
- More moisture stays in the soil because it is not exposed to evaporation, so at least do not dig between April and September.

However, apart from remedying soil structure, digging is helpful in exposing soil-borne pests to hungry birds, and in getting down to the roots of perennial weeds. Other than that, the choice is largely down to how much you enjoy it or not.

If dig it you will, spades, forks, muscles and bones are best. Mechanical cultivators have their place, but do not help you to pick out weeds, break up the subsoil or incorporate organic matter deep down. All-important requirements for the water-efficient garden, these are best achieved through double digging. Then after time to recover, and the soil to settle, you can prepare the surface. In some cases this may be all that is needed: forking over and knocking out lumps, raking, treading and levelling.

Double digging is hard work and a bit old fashioned, but if the subsoil is compacted or panned in some way, the extra effort will help plant roots grow deeper and access more moisture. The topsoil is turned over to one spade depth and the subsoil beneath broken up with a fork to the same depth again. Single digging is the same process without forking over the subsoil. In each case organic matter can be mixed into the topsoil, perhaps by spreading it over the surface before you start.

Lightly forking in shovel loads of grit or compost can help relieve drainage problems, not only by altering texture or structure, but also by raising the soil surface. More distinguished, higher raised beds, made from railway sleepers, and bricks and so on, will make for easier stoop-free gardening and can be filled with soil to suit the plants you want to grow – rich organic material, perhaps for vegetables, or sharply drained grits and gravels for xerophytes. Even more drastic would be a piped drainage system, which, cleverer still, could be used to harvest water. Lawns intended for winter use and vegetable plots are possible candidates for piped drainage, but otherwise it is easier, and more sensible really, just to choose plants that suit the conditions you've got.

Growing acid loving plants on a chalky soil is another case of making things difficult. It's an uphill struggle, but there are plenty of other things you can grow (*see* page 144) so best stick to them. Liming the soil for lime-loving plants is easier though. In vegetable crops it is routinely done to neutralize acidity and so maintain soil fertility.

Use of fertilizers, especially phosphorus, when preparing the ground can often help to aid plant establishment. But the best thing to do by far in most situations is apply loads of muck. Municipal green waste, manure and mushroom compost are all possible sources of bulky organic matter, and of course you can make your own (*see* page 148). Dug in deep or laid on the surface for worms to take down, it brings so many benefits. Just shovel it on, because if there is one golden rule of water-efficient gardening, then that is it.

Planting, sowing and getting them going

If there were other golden rules, then 'plant in the dormant season' would be up there as well. October to March is what you should aim for, as long as the soil is not frozen or saturated. Autumn is generally best, because it allows some root growth to be made before any drought conditions occur the following summer. Where winter waterlogging could be a problem though, spring planting would work better. Planting between May and August should really be avoided, because it will almost definitely create unnecessary watering. Similar principles apply when moving plants from one place to another. Deciduous ones should be leafless, and evergreens, if possible, should be moved in September or late April. The warm soil temperatures then cause quick root growth that is soon able to compensate for the inevitable water loss. The soil should be moist when the plants are lifted, and there should be as much of it as possible, and well attached to the roots.

Once you've got plants in from a nursery, your duty of care begins. Container-grown plants, particularly if in leaf, should be placed where they can be easily watered. Treat root-balled plants likewise, though these can dry out from the sides as well, so should be packed together or protected as necessary. Bare-root plants should be unwrapped and 'heeled in', that is, with their roots securely covered in moist soil or compost so as not to dry out.

Planting into beds of well prepared ground is fairly straightforward, because all the hard work is done. The ground should be moist and the roots as well, with the uppermost ones just barely covered by the soil surface. Gentle but firm consolidation around the roots ensures they have good contact with the soil but are not so packed in that they can't breathe. These basic requirements also apply when planting a specimen into unprepared ground.

Another thing to try, at the planting stage, is to treat the plant with special fungi that can live in or on its roots as mycorrhizae, and really help in the uptake of water and nutrients. Products containing these fungi can be bought in garden centres and sprinkled into the planting hole or used as a root dip. Plantings on disturbed soils, such as new housing developments, are likely to benefit most from this treatment.

The establishment period

As soon as a plant is planted, its establishment period begins. The crucial formative period of upbringing, during which, if all goes well, it becomes a strong independent happy and well-adjusted individual. Size and age at the time of planting are critical here (*see* page 26). The bigger and older a plant is, the more water it will need to get going, and the longer the period over which it needs that help. So 'plant young and small' is another golden rule, and you

PLANTING A SPECIMEN INTO UNPREPARED GROUND

The method of pit planting is commonly used for planting specimen trees into lawns but may also be used for shrubs in a border if the whole area is not to be dug (*see* page 125). These are the key points from a water-efficient point of view:

- Backfill mainly with topsoil that came from the pit – adding organic matter will improve the soil, but it should not be used to replace it.
- Ensure that the soil around the roots is gently firmed but not compacted, and that it's in good contact with the roots.
- Use an irrigation pipe around the roots to help get water and air to them.
- Secure the tree well to a stake, so its roots do not move around when trying to establish.
- Water the tree in, if it has leaves of any sort, and unless you're absolutely sure it's going to rain.
- Mulch over the surface and ensure no weeds or grass grow within 50cm (18in) of the trunk.

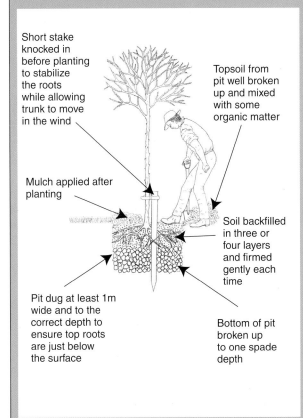

Short stake knocked in before planting to stabilize the roots while allowing trunk to move in the wind

Topsoil from pit well broken up and mixed with some organic matter

Mulch applied after planting

Soil backfilled in three or four layers and firmed gently each time

Pit dug at least 1m wide and to the correct depth to ensure top roots are just below the surface

Bottom of pit broken up to one spade depth

Planting a bare-root tree.

- Keep the roots moist all the time before planting.
- Fork over the sub-soil as you would in double digging.
- Consider using a mycorrhizal product to make the roots more effective.

A piece of perforated drainpipe, or proprietary tree irrigation system, can be coiled around the roots to help with watering.

The same principles would apply to a container tree, although the roots would not be able to go around the stake. An angled stake or two stakes with a cross-bar would usually be used instead.

For smaller shrubs and perennials, the irrigation pipe may be substituted simply by embedding a plastic flower pot into the soil next to the plant, for watering into. In the same way, planting into a slight depression can help direct water to the roots, but on anything other than a really well-drained soil this could cause waterlogging. If drainage is bad, a mound may be better, with the pot as well, to catch water in summer.

can't get plants any younger or smaller than at their embryo stage. These are the ones in seeds, which if you sow direct, are surely the most water efficient way of introducing plants to a garden. Give them a nice moist soil, to trigger germination, then the water demand of the growing baby plant stays more or less in balance with its own supply. By not restricting or disturbing the roots in any way, you will have given it the best chance possible of surviving on natural rainfall. OK, it could grow much better if watered, but it will probably not be a matter of life or death, as it often is for uprooted or container grown nursery youngsters.

You will often hear the phrase 'drought-resistant once established', inferring that a plant needs a bit of help to get started but after that it will find its own water. How long this takes will depend on various things: the type and condition of nursery stock, the quality of ground preparation, the care of the plant before planting and how well it is planted. Then the better the care during this period, the sooner the plant will reach a stage when routine maintenance will suffice – hopefully just a bit of weeding, pruning, and an annual mulch.

But water is the priority for anything that has just been planted, and how it has adapted to cope with drought in the long term will give clues as to how needy it will be early on. It's the roots that are the problem – they may be damaged and in short supply. At best the roots just haven't begun to explore the soil yet, so until they really get growing, the plant needs to save water. If it has small, waxy or leathery wilt-proof leaves, that's good. If the leaves are larger and look like they will wilt or shrivel, then it relies more on its roots and their ability to access water from far and wide. At this point the roots cannot do this, so the need for help will be greater, and if it's a big old plant, even greater still.

The aim is to ensure the plant stays healthy enough to get its roots growing out into the soil and finding their own water. Its root zone must be wetted often enough, and over a sufficiently long period, to achieve this. Keeping the plant barely alive is better than having it die, but doesn't further its progress. Stress from drought will seriously impair a young plant's development, and you won't necessarily see it wilt dramatically. Sparse foliage, and leaves undersized, brown at the tips, or slightly drooping – these are all signs of quiet desperation in a young tree or shrub. You could look for the very first signs and water then, or you could adopt a routine for the establishment period. There comes a time when the roots can manage on their own, as long as they really are on their own, and not in competition with other plants. Then in many cases, such as hedges, ground cover and specimen

Grass acts like a weed around the roots of young trees, competing aggressively for water.

trees, the stage is reached when the plants can cope entirely themselves. Your work then is done, or at least the nurturing bit. Attention turns to controlling the beast.

Some plants of course never completely grow up; they are poor competitors, or don't suit the site, so need pampering for ever. They still have a crunch period though, of intensive care, before the routine of weeding and occasional watering kicks in. You don't want to be watering weeds, of course, and the need for weeding will normally extend beyond the need for watering.

Controlling pests too, may be a special requirement for young plants. They can reach a stage of not succumbing to rabbits and slugs, but early protection is vital. Checking guards and supports, as well as feeding in spring, may all be additional tasks for the establishment phase. And last but not least, mulching. The mainstay of plant establishment, mulching seriously lessens the need to weed and water, and can feed the plants too.

With all things done well, a standard tree in a lawn, a hedge and a bank of ground cover should all be fully established in two to three years. Perennials and small shrubs in mixed borders would take a year or two. And a summer bedding display should be fairly independent after six weeks.

USES OF PLANTS

Hedges and windbreaks

It would be unusual to sow a hedge direct but not totally ridiculous. Plants such as hornbeam (*see* page 65) and field maple (*see* page 42) make great hedges and could be grown from seed outside. Hedges are a crucial part of the garden structure though, and often the first soft landscape component to go in; we can't help but want them large and doing their thing straight away. But small plants are best, particularly in this situation. The aim is not for a single plant but for a group of plants with a single identity. Young vigorous ones will knit together and achieve this far more quickly and effectively than the older ones we often choose for instant screening and privacy.

Complete freedom from competition is important too. Make sure you keep a good strip of ground for the hedge, at least about 80cm (2ft 4in) wide, cleared of grass and weeds. The full job would be to remove the topsoil, dig over the subsoil, place the hedging plants, backfill with topsoil and organic matter and then mulch. One row of plants at 50cm (20in) spacings along the centre of the strip should be enough. Larger evergreens could go further apart, and dwarf hedging closer together. If that all sounds too involved and you're looking to compromise, the weed clearing and mulch are the most important bits, apart from the plants. But you do want the hedge to grow quickly up, to its intended height, so the more you can do to prepare for it, the better.

If ever there was a perfect opportunity in gardens for drip irrigation (*see* page 150) it must be this, with the plants nicely lined up in a row. Where big leafy plants are used for instant screening on exposed windy sites, anti-transpirant sprays can be helpful. They block the stomata, reducing water loss for a few weeks while the roots get established. Another option for reducing transpiration is the temporary use of artificial windbreaks.

Bare-root deciduous plants sold for hedging will usually be better and bushier if cut back by half before they start growing. But most hedges don't need pruning until they extend beyond the width and height you want. Then thickened by repeated clipping, they make more solid 'walls' around us, and denser tangles for nesting birds.

Planted windbreaks are like hedges, but allowed to grow taller and taller and usually comprised of a deciduous and evergreen mix. This reduces any effect of turbulence and protects a larger area, on the leeward side, from the strength and drying power of wind. Fairly upright trees like holly (*see* page 60) and alder (*see* page 42) work well, planted a good stride or more apart.

Lawns and other grassy areas

England is green and pleasant in summer only when there is enough water for grass leaves to stay alive. Otherwise it's brown, and far less pleasant, leading us to question whether a lawn is the most sensible surface for our gardens. There is nothing better, it's true, for lying around, rolling about and playing games on, but if these are not your priorities, then maybe it's time for a change. Gravel, paving or a drought resistant ground cover all spring to mind, none of which would need quite the care and attention of a nice green lawn.

But if it's a lawn you want, and water-efficient too, there are ways and means, and they may include sprinklers. When water is scarce, spraying it around to simulate rain is clearly wasteful. Let the grass go brown, because when real rain comes it will green up again and the water you've got can be used on food crops or plants that would die without it. Brown lawns are ugly though, and they will take no wear and tear, so sprinklers, if permitted, may not be completely beyond the pale. But they would need to be used very carefully though, and only when needed, getting the right amount of water to the right place with minimal wastage. A built-in automatic system could be designed and set to achieve this, but for most of us tempted in this way, we would have to indulge ourselves with the sprinkler on a hose pipe (*see* page 149).

There are alternatives to sprinklers though, far more water efficient and less demanding of your careful attention to timing and placement. Least compromising of the green carpet effect is to start a new lawn using different species. Seed mixes and turf are comprised of various lawn grasses, some more drought tolerant than others. Fescues

PLANTS FOR HEDGES

Hedges can be formal neatly shaped, clean-cut green walls, or more laid back in varying degrees. Formal ones, especially those with small leaves, are crisp and simple in outline, ideally narrowing towards the top. They give a hard edge to soft, loose mixed plantings, through their strength and uniformity – qualities that rely on a good sturdy upbringing of each plant in the hedge. So efforts in ground preparation, weeding and watering are especially fruitful. Suitable plants for formal hedges include:

Buxus sempervirens
Carpinus betulus
Elaeagnus × ebbingei
Griselina littoralis
Ilex aquifolium
Ligustrum ovalifolium
Lonicera nitida
Photinia × fraseri
Pittosporum tenuifolium
Prunus cerasifera 'Pissardii'
Prunus laurocerasus
Taxus baccata

The ancient box hedge at Copyhold Hollow B&B. Too old to be strictly formal, it probably hasn't been watered for several centuries.

Informal hedges are pruned for a more natural shape and for seasonal display of flower or fruit. There is a far wider choice than for formal hedging, but the following are good examples:

Berberis × stenophylla
Ceanothus 'Dark Star'
Cotoneaster simonsii
Escallonia rubra
Hebe salicifolia
Hippophae rhamnoides
Myrtus communis
Olearia × haastii
Physocarpus opulifolius
Pyracantha Saphyr range
Rosa rugosa
Tamarix tetrandra

Rosa rugosa rose is one of the best shrubs for an informal flowering and almost impenetrable hedge.

For the English rural hedgerow effect, and all it has to offer your local wildlife, you could use a mixture of wild plants such as hawthorn, spindle, holly and field maple.

Another type of hedge you might want to include is a dwarf one, coming up to little more than knee height. Most famously, this would be a box hedge of formal appearance, though *Ilex crenata* 'Convexa' and *Euonymus japonicus* 'Microphyllus' could perhaps be used instead. But dwarf hedges can be loose and flowery too, using herbs such as lavender or hyssop, as well as low growing cultivars of ornamental shrubs like *Potentilla* and *Philadelphus*.

are among the best under dry conditions, particularly one called rhizomatous tall fescue (RTF). With deep searching roots, it finds its own water and forms a reasonably dense, hard-wearing lawn. Another option is to use a seed mix containing tiny leaved 'microclover'. It stays green and mingles amongst the grass without the clumpy effect you get from weed clover.

Sowing a new lawn is less demanding of water than laying turf. Sowing should be done in the warmer months of autumn or spring. If you do lay turf, autumn is usually best. The familiar sight of newly laid turves curling up at the edges should be enough to remind you not to do that in late spring or summer.

Mulching mowers are a good idea. They chop up the clippings and disperse them amongst the grasses, recycling nutrients and helping retain moisture in the lawn. Increasing the height of cut up to about 50mm (2in) is important in dry conditions. More leaves means better root growth, helping with water uptake, and the less disturbance grass gets when it's stressed, the better.

Autumn lawn care

How you care for an established lawn is crucial. If you really do care, and don't want to just mow it, then the normal programme of autumn lawn care can help a lot. Feeding in spring and summer with nitrogen-rich fertilizers is not helpful, because the grass grows green and lush, needing lots of water to stay that way. Autumn lawn feed, with higher levels of potassium, would be better to use even in spring, if you are expecting a hot dry summer. Applying a wetting agent may be worthwhile to help the lawn absorb rainfall and any irrigation you give it.

Early autumn is the time for a lot of the special care that needs to be given to nice fine lawns. Much of the work involved will help the lawn recover from the previous summer and give it a fighting chance of surviving the next. These are the tasks:

Feeding: Give a light feed with an autumn fertilizer to help the grass recover from summer.

Scarifying: Scratch the lawn severely using a spring-tined rake or a mechanical scarifier. This reduces the build-up of thatch, that tangled organic layer at the base of the grass plants. If thatch gets much more than about 10mm (½in) thick, it

impedes the downward movement of water and exposes the grass roots within it to drying out.

Aerating: Spike the lawn using a garden fork, a special hollow-tined fork or a special spiking machine. The deep holes it creates, up to about 15cm (6in) apart, allow air and water get to the roots.

Top-dressing: Brush special mixtures of organic matter and free-draining sand into the grass and down the holes made by aerating. On clayey soils you would use more sand, allowing water to percolate down, and on sandy soils, more organic matter to help retain moisture. Apply the mix evenly at about 5kg per sq m (10 lb per sq yd) and work it in with the back of a rake.

Re-seeding: Use a rake to rough up bare patches and re-seed them with a grass seed mix containing at least 50 per cent fescues.

Wildflower meadow

You will be cutting the grass less often anyway, when it's not growing so much due to lack of water, and if your heart warms to the rougher look and easier lifestyle, just leave it alone altogether. A few weeks without mowing will see weeds turning to wildflowers, and being more drought resistant they stay green much longer than the grass. A mown path will reassure loved ones that you haven't completely lost the plot, and you may want to go one step further by turning your lawn into a wildflower meadow. But even if wildflowers for you can only ever be weeds, lawn herbicides should not be used during dry conditions, as they will only put the grass into greater despair.

Wildflowers thrive in meadows where the soil is too poor for grasses to grow strongly and smother them. Then when the 'hay' is cut, leaving gaps for flowers to seed into, they continue to flourish and spangle the soft grassy meadow with summer colour. It sounds simple, and it can be, but in gardens the soil is often too rich, and the wrong kind of plants take hold – coarse weeds and grasses, bullying out the prettier wildflowers. Stony, sandy, chalky and even clay soils, not enriched with manures or fertilizers, are ideal. They will dry out in the summer, favouring wildflowers like yarrow (*see* page 81), black knapweed (*see* page 91) and lady's bedstraw (*see* page 117), which can all survive well amongst grasses in a range of conditions.

Yarrow, black knapweed and lady's bedstraw are all at home here in a dry flowery meadow.

You can sow both wildflowers and grass seed mixes onto prepared ground, or just sow wildflowers and let the grasses find their way in. Alternatively, small plants can be introduced into grass that is already there. But you do need to choose the right species for the particular soil texture and microclimate you've got. Very weedy weeds like thistles and nettles might need controlling with herbicides first, but if they are really a problem, it's an ominous sign that the soil is too fertile and that drastic measures are needed to make a meadow successful. Stripping away say 10cm (4in) depth of topsoil and putting it somewhere else, perhaps on your kitchen garden, may seem mad, but it would work. The vegetables would root deeper and grow better with less irrigation, and the wildflowers would be delighted.

If the conditions are right, maintenance for a meadow is minimal. Cutting in April and October is a good idea, with the main 'hay making' in early August. Raking up the cut grass is really important, but it's all good stuff for the compost heap and then the vegetable patch. So the rich gets richer and the poor gets poorer, but in this case it's good.

Ground cover

An alternative to lawn is a simple planting of ground cover. Not nearly so good for walking or playing on, but you won't have to mow it, and it gives different effects of colour and texture. There are many species amongst ground cover plants that resist drought far better than lawn grasses, and many amongst these that grow in the shade. Sunny banks that are hard to mow, and dry soil under trees where the lawn always struggles – these are typical sites for ground cover. But you could plant it anywhere and do away with the mower. Steep banks present problems for ground cover so special methods for planting on slopes will need be looked at (*see* page 133).

Once properly established, a simple ground cover of just one species will require very little maintenance until the plants decline with old age. No mulching, no watering except in extreme drought, perhaps a bit of weeding, depending on how thickly and how tall the plants grow, and occasional pruning.

Taller emergent plants can be included to create more interest, but if the scheme gets too complex, with lots of different plants, the demands for maintenance get higher. Territorial squabbles occur between plants, and weeds grow in gaps because the cover is not uniform. Plants need attention at different times, and what you've got is a mixed planting, with all the fun and hard work it entails. There's nothing wrong with that. Covering the ground, at least in the summer, is something to aim for in most plantings, low maintenance or not. Unless conditions are really harsh, like on a hot Mediterranean hillside, it's natural for vegetation to cover the ground, and of course it makes maximum use of the rain you get.

Osteospermum and geranium ground cover combine with ceanothus and purple-leaved prunus to make a simple low-maintenance mixed planting.

GROUND COVER PLANTS

Ground cover needs to smother weeds, so plants must be chosen which, in your conditions, will thrive and grow densely. They will want a head start, so any weeds already there must first be banished. Then you plant closely together to cover the ground as quickly as possible. 30cm (12in) apart suits little carpeters like thyme, while larger shrubs like junipers can go at 1m/yd spacings. Most others do perfectly well at 45–60cm (18–24in) apart. With lots of plants and lots of roots you will need lots of water, so mulching is a must in the establishment phase, until the plants mulch themselves.

Ground cover plants can be evergreen or deciduous and woody or not; so long as they stay low enough to look down on, and dense enough to claim the ground as their own without too much help. All of the following, and many others, can do this when planted close together as a group.

Woody species
Artemisia 'Powis castle'
Brachyglottis 'Sunshine'
Ceanothus 'Blue Mound'
Cistus × pulverulentus 'Sunset'
Cotoneaster dammeri★
Erica carnea
Euonymus fortunei 'Emerald Gaiety'★
Genista lydia
Hebe rakaiensis
Hedera hibernica★
Hypericum calycinum★
Juniperus squamata 'Blue carpet'
Lonicera pileata★
Salvia officinalis 'Purpurascens'
Santolina chamaecyparissus

Non-woody species
Acaena microphylla
Armeria maritima
Asplenium scolopendrium★
Bergenia cultivars
Erigeron glaucus
Euphorbia amygdaloides var. *robbiae*★
Geranium macrorrhizum★
Helictitrichon sempervirens
Liriope muscari★
Nepeta × faassenii
Osteospermum jucundum
Pennisetum alopecuroides 'Hameln'
Stachys byzantina
Thymus pseudolanuginosus
Vinca minor★

★= Plants that will form ground cover in shade under trees

Planting on a slope

Steep sloping banks bring fun and interest to gardens, but additional problems too. Though steps and retaining walls can help, there is usually a need to get plants growing. Grass can be tricky to mow, so ground cover planting makes good sense. It controls erosion, brings colour and texture, and once established, will require only a minimal amount of clambering around. But ground preparation, planting, mulching and watering are fraught with difficulties in this battle against gravity.

Plant selection needs careful thought too. Banks are often particularly dry, because water runs off them and not into them. They may also present extremes of hot and sunny, or cool and shady, and often consist of heavily compacted clay subsoil, moulded to shape by a digger's bucket.

If there is already a dense cover of rough grass or weeds, treat it with herbicide, then cut back the dense stems but leave the roots intact to help retain the soil. Serious digging should be avoided, but wiggling a garden fork to its full depth can assist penetration by roots and water. Planting small, in say 1-litre containers, helps to reduce the need for soil disturbance and is a must if you elect to plant through a membrane. Removing soil and putting it back through a hole in fabric is awkward enough on flat ground.

Climbing plants such as ivy, which attach to flat surfaces, can be planted at the top and bottom of very steep slopes with strict instructions to meet in the middle. Otherwise you can plant straight into the bank, preferably in autumn, and with a bit of luck and wet weather you may not need to water. If you really think you will have to water, then little terraces will help, perhaps retained by rocks or railway sleepers (see page 134).

Mixed plantings

Most of the planting in most of our gardens is shrubs and perennials combined together for ornamental display. There may be quite a mix, and they all need to be happy so you have to make sure that each plant suits the place. That way, far less is needed to make the place suit the plants – just dealing with obvious shortcomings like perennial

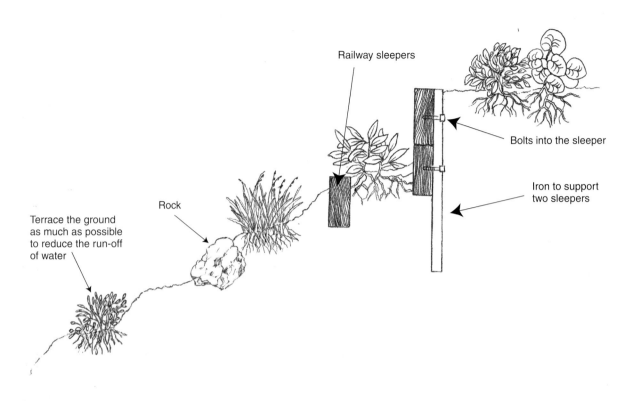

Railway sleepers

Bolts into the sleeper

Iron to support
two sleepers

Rock

Terrace the ground
as much as possible
to reduce the run-off
of water

Planting on a slope.

weeds, bad soil structure or a light soil colour that screams out for muck.

Conditions can often be difficult at the base of walls, so wall shrubs and climbers may need extra attention, but depth and richness of soil is particularly important for herbaceous perennials. It's a big task, to arise anew from the ground each year, especially for a plant expected to find its own water, and when there are a lot being planted, for full summer lushness, it's best not to compromise on ground preparation – double digging, and barrow loads of anything rich, dark, weed free and available.

If it's mainly shrubs going in, and largish ones at any more than a stride apart, then you could plant each one separately, like a specimen tree without the stake. This represents a kind of no-dig approach (*see* page 125) and is quite feasible when soil structure is all right. You would still need to get rid of weeds or grass from the whole bed, then mulch over the top to conceal the short cut and for all the other more noble reasons.

Membranes too could be used here, where a few large plants rather than lots of little plants are going in. The fewer the cuts in the fabric, the simpler the job of planting through it, and the less opportunities there are for weeds to grow. But be cautious! If the soil is heavy, and at all prone to waterlogging, the membrane will exacerbate this and cause real problems to many plants. Freely drained soils, with sparse plantings of suitable species, are one situation where membranes can help. Covered with gravel or some other aggregate, they give the right look, and are a low maintenance answer for a part of the garden that you don't want to garden.

Mixed plantings generally need a fair bit of gardening. Mulching, weeding and watering in the establishment phase soon becomes a routine of pruning and other tasks. There will be more mulching and weeding for sure, but watering hopefully only when you have moved or replaced something.

Wall shrubs and climbers

Training plants up walls and over other garden structures gives vertical greenness without using up space, and with many species it's the treatment they want. Natural climbers almost expect it. Their stems are specially adapted to climb up other plants or over rock faces, so in gardens they help ensure that you've got a plant growing in every place possible: over a shed, up a wall, through a tree, and if there's nothing to climb on they'll scramble over the ground. Of course maximum use of space means maximum use of water; you will need all you can get, but it won't be wasted.

There are many free-standing shrubs that also benefit from the protection of a wall or just look tidier with their backs to a wall. Unlike climbers, wall shrubs like this don't aspire to reach for the sky so are often better choices for the modest vertical surfaces offered by fences and garages. But the ground where we plant them is often quite dry, perhaps sheltered from rain carried on westerly winds,

---

SHRUBS AND CLIMBERS FOR WALLS

For a north or east facing wall the best choices are tough hardy plants with a low light requirement:

Cotoneaster horizontalis
Euonymus fortunei 'Silver Queen'
Garrya elliptica
Hedera helix
Lonicera japonica 'Halliana'
Parthenocissus quinquefolia
Pyracantha cultivars

For a south or west facing wall, these species from warmer sunnier habitats are particularly happy. They will need good drainage too, especially since they are likely to receive a good deal of the available rain.

Abutilon megapotamicum
Carpenteria californica
Cytisus battandieri
Fremontodendron californicum
Lathyrus latifolius
Robinia hispida
Rosa banksiae
Sophora tetraptera
Wisteria floribunda

---

or sucked dry by concrete and builder's rubble. So make the most of a wall that bears the full blast of the rain and choose carefully for walls that don't, preparing well with a good deep pit of enriched soil if necessary. Install wall fixings for support before planting, and place the plant a boot length away, sloping back to the wall so it knows your intentions.

Dividing and transplanting herbaceous perennials

Dividing and transplanting means lifting perennials and splitting them up into smaller pieces of young fresh growth, each with roots and buds, then replanting them into freshly prepared ground. This is sometimes something the herbaceous perennials need, but normally something we do for fun. It brings change to a border from year to year, almost like adding new plants, and done in the dormant season as it normally is, does not put too much extra demand on water.

Some such as *Achillea*, *Aster* and *Coreopsis* need it regularly, every three years or so, in order to maintain good displays. Many others, such as *Alchemilla*, *Geranium* and most grasses, don't so much need it but are quite happy to be split up for new plants or just for tidying and starting anew.

There are many drought-resistant perennials however that do not really like it, and are best left alone. This accords with the observation that plants adapted to difficult growing conditions don't take kindly to being disturbed, particularly ones with deep or fleshy taproots such as *Aquilegia*, *Baptisia*, *Eryngium*, *Gypsophila*, *Linum Oenothera* and *Papaver*. You will find them difficult to divide into viable pieces by the normal methods of pulling apart with hand or forks, or chopping through with something sharp.

The dormant season is best for dividing perennials, with early spring the safest time for most species. If you simply want a small number of new plants from a clump that doesn't need dividing, then it is often best not to lift it but just to chop a piece out with a spade and fill in the hole with some soil. The piece of the clump remaining in the soil will not have its roots disturbed so should be all right for water.

Seasonal displays

Annuals and biennials can bring extra change and boosts of colour to mixed displays, but they may also be given their own special beds, altered from winter to summer, in accord with your whim. Whether planted or sown, in autumn, spring or summer, they need a fair bit of effort. Stripping out the old stuff, and a good thorough weed, then digging over, adding compost, or maybe a dressing of fertilizer, before planting or sowing anew. Twice a year you may do this, which is pretty serious pottering about; high input, high output, with a water demand to match. But it's planting half-hardies in early summer that is the worst offender. Proximity to water butts and lots of organic matter are mitigating circumstances, and if you do it by autumn planting and sowing direct, all the better.

Annual toadflax, shirley poppies and cornflowers feature in this direct-sown annual seed mix from Pictorial Meadows. (Photo: Evan Giles)

Wallflowers and forget-me-nots sown into a nursery bed, or a spare part of the vegetable patch, in early summer can be moved to the display bed in autumn and interplanted with tulips. It might look a bit 'public park', but nothing could be cheerier in spring, and neither you nor a nurseryman will have been watering containers all summer. Stripping this out in May will not be too late for a direct sowing of summer annuals, and there are some excellent seed mixes available, for natural meadow-like colour right through to autumn.

But if it's a more traditional summer display you want, selecting the most drought resistant bedding and container plants is the first step. Then ensure a good depth of soil, moisture retentive but porous, qualities which are even more important with containers and baskets. Container plants are completely dependent on you. They only get what you give them, and they cannot escape from it. Have the container as big as possible, so the roots can forage at least for a while, but be careful not to drown them. Don't scrimp on the compost you use. A good quality container compost works best, and 'John Innes' mixed in helps a lot too, though it may be too heavy for hanging baskets. Water retaining gels also reduce the need to water so frequently, as does mulching over the top with some kind of aggregate. Baskets with water reservoirs and water retaining liners are additional features of container gardening armoury, and you need to do what you can, because baskets and pots, above all in the garden, are the biggest water spenders, unless of course you sprinkle the lawn.

The kitchen garden

Flowery pots and green lawns can certainly make high demands on water, but so too can the kitchen garden. Though perhaps less wasteful, and probably more noble, to feed the body and not just the spirit extra water will often be needed to get really good yields from most vegetables. So if you are a serious kitchen gardener, aiming to feed yourself and family with essential food crops for much of the year, you may well compromise on lawn and flowers.

Less ambitious, recreational veg growing for fun and good exercise is more dispensable in a hot dry summer, and the exuberant potager style on the normal home garden scale rarely contributes more than accessories to the family table. Like the modern cottage garden, it will not make the difference between feast and famine that it would have of old, so is best regarded as an additional theme to mixed borders or containers.

A dedicated place, carefully selected and as big as possible, is the efficient way with vegetables, getting maximum return from your labour and resources such as water.

BEDDING AND CONTAINER PLANTS

For summer/autumn

Although many of the following can be sown direct, they are all fairly drought resistant even if bedded out as small pot-grown plants in early summer. This is just a selection. Any others listed as annuals (*see* page . . .) could be used in bedding displays or containers.

Agastache rugosa
Aptenia cordifolia★
Brachyscome iberidifolia★
Calendula officinalis
Convolvulus tricolor
Cosmos bipinnatus
Dorotheanthus bellidiformis
Felicia bergeriana★
Gazania hybrids
Lavatera trimestris
Lobularia maritima
Pennisetum setaceum 'Rubrum'
Phyllostachys suworowii
Portulaca grandiflora★
Salvia farinacea
Sanvitalia procumbens★
Tagetes patula
Zinnia elegans
★= Good for hanging baskets, mainly because of their trailing stems.

For winter/spring

Far fewer bedding plants are available for winter and spring display and, planted as they are in autumn, drought resistance is far less of an issue. The following are good examples, but others, such as the popular pansies, and polyanthus, could also be used with little or no watering.
Bellis perennis
Erysimum cheiri
Matthiola incana
Myosotis sylvatica
Tulipa hybrids

Bulbs and wallflowers – simple spring cheer at no cost of water.

For permanent display

Containers can also be planted for permanent display, often with evergreens such as *Buxus sempervirens* and *Laurus nobilis* pruned into shapes, or with exotic foliage plants like *Phyllostachys nigra* and *Chamaerops humilis*. In others, such as *Callistemon citrinus* and *Agapanthus africanus*, attractive foliage is combined with flowers.

Whether out in the garden, or on an allotment, there are two basic systems for vegetable growing: in rows across the entire plot, or in beds separated by paths. The traditional way is in rows, with the tending of the plants, and weed control, done from between these rows. The regular hoeing that this involves may help retain moisture in the soil by leaving a dusty mulch, but the damage inflicted on the surface roots of vegetables would seem to counteract this advantage.

Weed control through mulching and hand pulling causes no such damage, and is better suited to the smaller spaces involved when you grow vegetables in beds. Heavily enriched with organic matter, and slightly raised, these beds give the optimum balance in water retention and drainage. They are narrow enough to ensure all work can be done from the paths between them, so they never get stood on and compacted. Not only your work, but also compost and other materials, including of course

Chives, an essential component of the ornamental potager.

all the water they get, and if the paths were impervious they could channel water to a rain garden planted with perennial food plants such as rhubarb, sorrel and lovage.

You can grow about the same amount of vegetables whichever system you use, but the beds can be built up rich and deep, for maximum water efficiency. Four beds works well for crop rotations, and they must be small enough to walk and work around. About 5 × 1.2m/yd is usually best.

The bed system makes it easy to operate a crop rotation, and works well also with the no-dig system (*see* page 123). This kind of gardening is fundamentally water efficient, underpinned by the same golden rule of applying organic matter. Beans and peas, the legume crops, rely on its water retaining properties, though if drought is likely, French beans are the ones to go for. Legumes help enrich the soil for brassicas, the cabbage family, which also thrive on lots of organic matter. The cabbage itself is not quite so dependent on water as are cauliflowers and Brussels sprouts, and the simple kales, which do not produce dense hearts, are the most drought resistant of all. Onions are similar, needing a well-enriched soil and plenty of moisture. Root crops are an exception, particularly

water, are directed exclusively at the ground where the crop is to grow, not at the ground that you walk on. The space apparently wasted on the paths is made up by the ability to grow vegetables closer together and more evenly spaced. The plants can completely cover the ground, making good use of

The arrangement of rows or beds in a plot – spacing of plants will depend on the kind of vegetable.

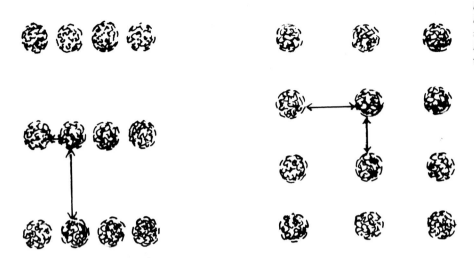

A comparison of the row and bed systems of planting – the bed system makes better use of the ground that you have carefully prepared and watered.

long-rooted carrots and parsnips, which do not form well where organic matter has been recently applied and which, by virtue of their taproots anyway, can cope with a degree of dryness.

A curly kale – better than cabbage if water is scarce

In fact several of our vegetables have drought resistant ancestry. Onions are thought to originate from wild plants of the mountains of central Asia, where their bulbs would have helped them survive

the dry season. The wild cabbage grows on coastal cliffs round Europe and the Mediterranean, and similarly the wild leek. But the cultivars we grow are different from their wild relatives, and we don't want them just to survive – we want them to grow quickly, big and lush and crisp, and that's why they need watering if the summer gets dry.

Fennel does not need much water if you just want its leaves, but the Florence variety does, if you want to enjoy the edible bulbs.

Rhubarb chard – ornamental, edible and drought-resistant.

The wild beet is another species of dry exposed coastal habitats round Europe. It has given rise to chard, perpetual spinach and beetroot, all of which are amongst the more drought resistant vegetables we can grow. Moreover, you can sow them direct and they will fit anywhere into a rotation.

The tomato family, including peppers, chillies and aubergines, and the cucumber family, with melons and pumpkins, are vegetables we grow for their fruit. All of these have a fairly low water demand for normal growth, but since they are grown as half-hardy annuals, planted outdoors in early summer, or into some kind of greenhouse growing system, they need watering anyway. Then, as with the other fruiting vegetables, peas, beans and sweet corn, water supply becomes most important during flowering and fruiting.

So watering during fruiting and flowering, when the crop most needs it, makes perfect sense in water-efficient vegetable gardening, and as with the fruiting vegetables, this is generally when the bit you want to eat is growing most rapidly. With potatoes it's when the tubers are developing, which generally starts when flowers form. With leafy vegetables like lettuce and cabbage, a constant supply

HERBS AND EDIBLE ORNAMENTALS

The following species are some of those that look nice and you can eat too.

Woody species
Acca sellowiana
Arbutus unedo
Aronia arbutifolia
Cercis siliquastrum
Elaeagnus angustifolia
Laurus nobilis
Myrtus communis
Olea europaea
Pinus pinea
Poncirus trifoliata
Rosmarinus officinalis
Salvia officinalis

Non-woody species
Agastache foeniculum
Calendula officinalis
Coriandrum sativum
Cynara scolymus
Foeniculum vulgare
Helianthus annuus
Hemerocallis fulva
Oenothera biennis
Origanum vulgare
Salvia sclarea
Silybum marianum

The salvia called clary: its leaves can be used in cooking, and its flowers for salads or tea.

GREENHOUSE GROWING

A greenhouse roof is enough of an obstacle to the water demands of crops like tomatoes and cucumbers, but having their roots restricted in grow bags or pots makes things much worse. Growing them each year in greenhouse soil leads to problems with pests and diseases, but there are ways to avoid this while still allowing a free root run.

Ring culture: This involves growing the plants in bottomless pots placed on top of a bed of mineral aggregate that drains freely but stays moist. The plants obtain most of their water by rooting down into the aggregate, but also retain fine fibrous feeding roots in the pot above. The aggregate needs to be kept separate from the soil and in winter could be left outside in porous containers so it is cleaned by the winter rain before re-use next year.

Straw bales: These are used to provide the searching root run for plants that are initially placed into ordinary compost on top of the moistened bale. As the plant grows the bale decomposes, generating some warmth and releasing nutrients and carbon dioxide. This process needs to be started by thoroughly soaking the bale, treating it with nitrogen fertilizer and allowing it to cool down before planting. It is a trickier system than ring culture, but fun to try if you are adventurous, and you get some good organic matter for the garden at the end.

You will still need to water with both these systems, though not nearly as frequently as with growbags, and of course careful attention to feeding is essential too. As soil-less methods, they are simple examples of the more high-tech hydroponic systems you can get, where plants are grown in a water/nutrient solution that is pumped around their roots. Although this may sound quite a watery thing, the water is recycled so it isn't wasteful.

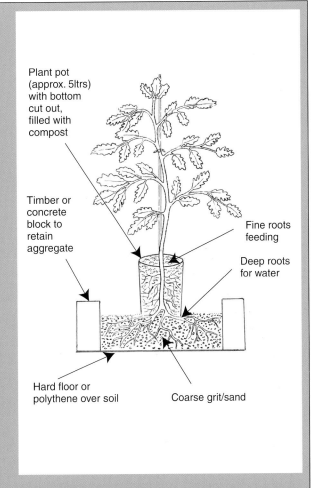

Plant pot (approx. 5ltrs) with bottom cut out, filled with compost

Timber or concrete block to retain aggregate

Fine roots feeding

Deep roots for water

Hard floor or polythene over soil

Coarse grit/sand

Ring culture – growing plants in bottomless pots placed on top of a bed of mineral aggregate.

of water is needed throughout, but it's when the dense hearts are developing that this is most critical, hence the relatively low water requirement of kale and open leafy salads, such as the Japanese mizuna and Chinese mustard. One particularly drought resistant leafy crop for cooking is New Zealand spinach. A spreading plant with succulent juicy leaves, it is treated as a half-hardy annual but can be sown direct in late spring.

If your time, space or capacity for work and watering are limited, and a vegetable patch is not a priority, then eat the shopping garnished with herbs and edible ornamentals from your garden displays. Most of these are perennials, a water-efficient plus, and some, such as seakale and asparagus, could well warrant a special bed of their own. This applies also to currants and berry fruit, not least because of the need to protect them from birds. They are woody perennials, so are fairly self-sufficient for water once established, though in dry summers they will yield better harvests if watered during fruit development. Good fertile soil and mulching are most important for fruit though, especially for apple trees on very dwarfing rootstocks that are inherently not very good at fending for themselves.

GARDEN CARE

Happy plants

Plants can suffer from pests and diseases, and also from disorders arising from too much or too little of the things they need. Water, of course, is one such thing, with short supply evident as wilting and other symptoms of drought stress (*see* page 28). Too much of it, not draining away, and the various signs of waterlogging can occur: leaves discoloured, yellow or brown, roots blackened and possibly rotting, leading to drought symptoms like wilting, die-back and stunted growth.

Weeds have their effect on plant health too, competing for water and nutrients with the plant you are trying to grow, and for light too if they get big enough. So plant health and happiness depends on a range of things that depend on each other, as can be seen from the various problems linked to drought and waterlogging.

Fertilizers must be used correctly, which means not at all in many cases, but they may well be necessary for plants in containers, or perhaps as a short term alternative to organic matter. Too much nitrogen makes plants soft and sappy, to the delight of aphids and fungal diseases too. So it must be balanced with the other nutrients, particularly potassium, which helps protect against pests and diseases and stresses like drought.

A plant growing well will be less susceptible to diseases than an unhappy struggler, and more able to survive the ravages of pests. Cultural control of pests, diseases and weeds, the foundation stone of good plant health, means good growing. The right plant for the right place, the right ground preparation, the right pruning, mulching and watering.

It's not just the amount of water that is important, but how much is applied, when and to where. Rain of course happens at any time and goes everywhere, soaking your plants from head to toe. But watering indiscriminately, apart from being wasteful, can damage your plants, especially if the water doesn't drain away.

Drought-resistance in heavy clay soils

Winter wetness is bad enough, but in summertime it can be even worse, because that's when plants need the most oxygen. There are drought resistant plants that can thrive in heavy clay soils, but many hate it, yearning for the arid, free draining conditions that their species evolved in. Most plants from wet boggy places can't stand drought, while some fussy ones, like daphnes, tread a tightrope between wet and dry, needing plenty of moisture but good drainage as well.

PLANTS FOR HEAVY CLAY SOILS

Most shrubs and perennials described under the following genera (*see* Chapter 3) are examples of plants that will grow in heavy clay. They require reasonable drainage but would tolerate waterlogging for limited periods.

Shrubs	Perennials
Abelia	*Achillea*
Aralia	*Agapanthus*
Aucuba	*Alchemilla*
Berberis	*Aster*
Buxus	*Bergenia*
Cotoneaster	*Calamagrostis*
Escallonia	*Centaurea*
Lonicera	*Cirsium*
Mahonia	*Coreopsis*
Philadelphus	*Echinacea*
Photinia	*Echinops*
Phyllostachys	*Geranium*
Physocarpus	*Helianthus*
Potentilla	*Hemerocallis*
Prunus	*Kniphofia*
Pyracantha	*Miscanthus*
Rosa	*Pennisetum*
Sambucus	*Vinca*

Salt-tolerance

It's not always simply a question of wet or dry. High levels of salt in the soil interfere with osmosis, inhibiting water uptake by plants, subjecting them to drought even when it's wet. Leaves scorch and drop, and stems die back, with similar symptoms occurring when there is salt spray in the air. Choose de-icing materials with care, and select salt-tolerant plants when necessary.

Salt and drought pose similar problems, and the strategies in plants to cope with them are similar too. Waxy and hairy leaves that are good for holding in water are also good for keeping out salt. Deep

SALT-TOLERANT PLANTS

Whether a plant will cope with salt or not is seldom for sure. It depends on severity and whether the salt is mainly dissolved in the soil or carried as spray on the wind. Most of the following shrubs and perennials (see Chapter 3 for details) are examples of plants that succeed close to the sea or where they might sometimes get splashed with de-icing salt.

Shrubs	Perennials
Artemisia	Achillea
Brachyglottis	Agapanthus
Convolvulus	Armeria
Elaeagnus	Centranthus
Escallonia	Erigeron
Garrya	Eryngium
Griselinia	Erysimum
Hebe	Eschscholzia
Juniperus	Foeniculum
Lavandula	Helictotrichon
Olearia	Iberis
Phlomis	Kniphofia
Pittosporum	Leymus
Rosa	Limonium
Rosmarinus	Osteospermum
Salvia	Phormium
Santolina	Sedum
Tamarix	Verbena

The vegetable seakale from shingle beaches is a real old salt.

roots keep plants stable in the face of strong salty winds and avoid high concentrations of salt that are splashed on the surface.

Problems linked to drought

As well as the more direct symptoms of drought (*see* page 128), lack of water can also lead to the following problems.

Powdery mildew: This is most likely to occur on drought-stressed plants with humid air round their tops. It is most commonly seen on the upper leaf surface but also elsewhere, as white powdery fungus, perhaps with growth distorted and dieback of stems. Pruning out diseased parts helps a lot, and keeping plants moist at the roots by timely mulching. Fungicides are effective but it's better to use resistant varieties where available.

Bolting: This is when vegetables, like beetroot and cabbage, start to flower and seed before they are ready to eat. There are different causes, but often it's lack of water or the shock of being transplanted. Plants think their time is up and are des-

perate to flower so they can pass on their genes. Resistant varieties are often available.

Flowering failure: Plants may want to flower but it's quite an effort and depends on water availability at the crucial time. Developing buds can just drop off or go brown and shrivel, though the plant remains healthy. Bulbs may be 'blind' due to drought earlier on, and flower stalks may shrivel and wilt as their blooms open. Moisture and mulching are important, but correct feeding may also be key.

Powdery mildew – usually worst when the soil is dry.

Calcium shortage: Dry soil is one of the causes of calcium shortage in plants, resulting in weakened growth and other symptoms such as scorching of young shoots and leaves. It is particularly a problem with food crops though, causing certain common disorders. Apple bitter pit shows as sunken brown spots in the skin and 'freckled' flesh with a bitter flavour. Blossom end rot occurs on tomatoes, the base of the fruit becoming tough leathery and brown in colour.

Splitting: When dry soil is wetted or temperature increases dramatically, food crops like carrots, celery, tomatoes and plums can split open. Maintaining a regular water supply is important, and when fruits are affected you should remove them so rot doesn't set in.

Leaf scorch: Leaf margins, and perhaps whole leaves, can go brown and crispy. Dry soil, as well as sun and wind can cause it, but so can wetness from too much rain or irrigation and bad drainage.

Effects of waterlogging

Ironically it is as if the plant is stressed by drought. And actually it is because the roots have drowned to death and can't take up water, so the leaves wilt, discolour, scorch and drop off. If the soil or compost is clearly saturated, then cease watering and improve drainage. Other effects to look out for are:

Oedema: Too much water and not enough transpiration can cause strange corky outgrowths under leaves and on stems. High humidity in greenhouses is a major cause, but reducing watering can certainly help.

Phytophthora: This fungus attacks the roots of trees and shrubs in wet badly drained soils. Top growth becomes yellow and sparse, but by this time the roots are in a pretty bad way, as evidenced by dark discolouration under the bark at the soil surface. Some species such as yew are most susceptible and would need removing with as much of the soil as possible. Improve the drainage as best as you can and replace with something more resistant, like hornbeam.

Problems linked to splashing water around

Splashing water about any more than needs be is not only wasteful but also causes damage to plants.

PLANTS FOR ACID OR ALKALINE SOILS

Soil pH is important, reducing nutrient uptake when it is too low or too high. Choosing plants for acid or alkaline soils is one way forward, but though the latter are often quite drought resistant, this is not the case with extreme acid lovers. Popular plants like rhododendrons and blueberries like their soil acid and moist; if you can give them that, they're happy as Larry and won't need your water because they've got their own. Here are some examples of plants which are tolerant of either high or low pH (for details *see* Chapter 3). Many of these are not fussy however, and don't necessarily depend on it.

Shrubs for acid soils

Berberis	*Ilex*
Cistus	*Indigofera*
Cotoneaster	*Juniperus*
Elaeagnus	*Lonicera*
Erica	*Physocarpus*
Genista	*Tamarix*

Shrubs for alkaline soils

Berberis	*Mahonia*
Buxus	*Olearia*
Cistus	*Philadelphus*
Cotoneaster	*Photinia*
Hebe	*Rosmarinus*
Hypericum	*Yucca*

Perennials for acid soils

Alchemilla	*Eryngium*
Aquilegia	*Hemerocallis*
Armeria	*Iris*
Bergenia	*Liriope*
Digitalis	*Ophiopogon*
Echinacea	*Pennisetum*

Perennials for alkaline soils

Achillea	*Gypsophilla*
Aquilegia	*Euphorbia*
Arabis	*Linum*
Asplenium	*Origanum*
Centranthus	*Thymus*
Dianthus	*Verbena*
Geranium	

Here are some of the problems caused by having wet leaves and a wet soil surface.

Downy mildew: This is a fungal disease of various vegetables and ornamentals such as hebes and wallflowers. Leaves die after first showing discoloured areas on their upper surface with a fluffy fungal growth beneath. It is encouraged by damp still conditions, so try to reduce the density of growth and avoid overhead watering. Remove infected leaves.

Grey mould: Also called botrytis, this is a very common fungal disease of all sorts of plants, appearing on their leaves fruits and flowers. Infected parts typically show a brown rot covered in fluffy grey mould. Relieve plant congestion, remove diseased parts as quickly as possible and avoid cool damp conditions, for example by not splashing water around late in the evening.

Smuts: These are fungal diseases of plants such as forget-me-nots and pot marigolds. Discoloured spots appear and spread across the leaves, causing serious damage. You have to destroy infected plants, and it stays in the soil so don't grow the same species there for a few years. Splashing water around spreads the spores to cause new infection, perhaps on self-sown seedlings of the previous plants.

Scorch: There are other causes of scorch (*see* page 144) but sometimes it results from hot sun shining onto water droplets on soft or hairy leaves. This causes pale patches that die. Avoid overhead watering, especially when hot sun is likely to occur soon afterwards.

Slugs: You are going to get them anyway, but you can discourage them a bit by timing and by placing your watering so the soil surface between plants isn't too wet at night.

Problems associated with particular plants

Crop rotation is cultural control, preventing the build-up of particular problems. Though inappropriate for most ornamentals, they can be treated so as to prevent any such problems from becoming too serious. This is done primarily by using as wide a range of plants as possible, year after year in seasonal displays and well mixed up throughout the garden so all the 'eggs' are not in any one 'basket', and some will attract the insects that eat the pests of the others. Resistant varieties too help a lot, especially for plants that suffer serial problems. Cultural methods like this are not always possible, but it helps when they are, and together with physical

and biological controls, should ensure pesticides are rarely needed.

Clubroot: This is a disease of the cabbage family, including wallflower, stocks, candytuft and honesty. The roots become swollen, distorted and dysfunctional, causing the tops to discolour and wilt through lack of water. It stays in the soil for many years and is brought into the garden on contaminated plants, tools and boots. Once in the soil, it can be controlled a bit by improving drainage, raising the pH and using strong healthy plants with well-formed roots. There are some fairly resistant vegetable varieties, but the simplest solution is to avoid the cabbage family in contaminated soil. There is no cure for infected plants. You just need to get rid of them. If when you look at the roots

Hypericum rust can be a real problem, but some varieties are more prone than others.

there are white maggots, it's cabbage root fly – no consolation for the plant in your hand but better news for future generations.

Fireblight: This bacterial disease affects certain members of the rose family such as firethorn, hawthorn and cotoneaster. The flowers wilt and die back along with young leaves and stems, giving an overall effect of scorching by fire. Small plants, if badly affected, will probably need completely removing, but otherwise you can stop the bacteria spreading too far by cutting way back into healthy wood and destroying the prunings. Fireblight is sometimes mistaken for pyracantha scab, which has a similar but less dramatic effect on the leaves and stems in early summer and then goes on to spoil the fruits.

Rust diseases: These tend to affect particular genera of garden plants. Rusty coloured deposits or pustules appear on the underside of leaves, with corresponding discolouration above. Removing infected parts, or whole plants, helps a lot but if a plant seems to suffer, it may be best to look for a more resistant variety or choose something completely different. Fungicides would need to be used regularly. Common rusts of drought resistant plants are those on hollyhock, juniper, mahonia and hypericum.

Box blight: Leaves of box turn black or brown and fall. In the most severe cases they go spotty first, and stems develop black streaking and die back. The fungi responsible can be seen under the leaves and thrive in wet weather, especially on densely clipped plants where air movement is poor. Pick up fallen leaves and remove infected stems quickly, because plants can recover though they may only be shadows of their former selves. There are no chemicals to cure this so do your best to ensure that infected plants or soil are not brought into the garden. These measures apply to holly blight too.

Leaf eating larvae: Different species of sawfly and moth can dramatically defoliate plants, giving them quite a shock and a fairly bleak look. Insecticides will be effective, it's true, but plants generally recover from the onslaught and birds will often help out. Picking the larvae off is not always ridiculous, as with the odd case of aquilegia sawfly and the colourful mullein moth on verbascum or buddleja. The recent cases of sawfly on *Berberis thunbergii* are pretty severe and may dissuade you from planting a whole hedge of that.

Rosemary beetle: This has appeared recently in England, decimating dry garden favourites like lavender and Russian sage. Off-white stripy larvae become metallic purple and green stripy adults, both feeding on leaves through the warmer times between autumn and spring. You can pick them off or shake them onto a sheet beneath. There are pesticides too, but be careful in choosing if you're planning to use a sprig of sage, rosemary or thyme in cooking. Vine weevil is related to beetles. Its grubs eat the roots of many species including sedum, and the adults make notches around the leaf edges of various shrubs. They are nasty things for sure, but an excellent biological control is available.

Sap suckers: This whole range of insects prefers a liquid lunch, piercing soft tissue of plants and tapping their fluid food supply. Growth is typically weakened and distorted, with plants getting sticky and covered in black sooty mould. More serious still, the insects may transmit viruses from one plant to another. Die-back in cypress and juniper may well be caused by conifer aphids. Strange swellings on young growth of hawthorn, firethorn, cotoneaster and apple trees will be from woolly aphids that hide under a fluffy white coating. Sucker insects are similar to aphids, with particular species affecting young shoots and leaves of their chosen victim – could be box, elaeagnus, bay or eucalypt. If there is sooty mould on the top of holly or euonymus leaves, there may well be cushion scale rigidly attached and busily sucking on the undersides of the leaves above. Depending on your priorities you may use pesticides, but sap suckers are an important link in the garden food chain.

Happy gardening

Scratching around amongst plants, with secateurs to hand, a small border fork and a bucket of compost captures the perfect oneness of garden and gardener. Weeds gently uprooted, mulch carefully placed and dead or tangly bits dealt with – what wonderful well being, and simple pleasures. It's even better perhaps if you've held back on the tidiness a little and chosen plants for wildlife, because insects and birds complete the picture.

Pruning

Pruning and weeding are the mainstays of gardening, and mulching for the water-efficient gardener is another essential. Pruning is done to take out growth that's damaged dead or diseased, to improve shape or reduce size and encourage the flaunting of finest assets: flowers, fruits, leaves and stems. It does have an impact on water usage, because fewer stems means fewer leaves, which in turn means less water loss. But fewer leaves also means less root growth, making plants less self-reliant, so where the fight for survival is really intense, pruning is only used as a last resort. Pruning back all leafy branches may be the difference between life and death for something newly transplanted or placed like a fish out of water in drought-ridden soil.

Many xerophytes though, from really dry habitats, don't like hard pruning even at the best of times. They are quite meek, timid plants actually, doing the best they can under difficult circumstances and can't be doing with dramatic events. It's worth noting, however, the species that do respond to severe pruning, because this is a useful technique in the water-efficient garden. Large shrubs, which you may want out, can often be pruned back hard, close to the ground, to start, revitalized, all over again. It's like getting a new shrub for nothing, with no need for planting or watering and without the trouble of fully exterminating the old one.

Some trees and shrubs are best pruned hard each year, to keep them to size and show off the best of their flowers or foliage. They respond with strong sturdy growth, resourced by deep searching roots, so they don't need the support and watering that may be necessary for similarly large herbaceous plants. This is a job for late winter or spring, so the plants respond quickly and have a whole season to grow. Summer pruning doesn't cause such carnage but is important for many spring and early summer flowering deciduous shrubs. Flowered stems are cut back, encouraging new green shoots lower down, to come up and flower next year.

Herbaceous stems are best cut back whenever you decide they have done their bit. Standing dead over winter, they can still look nice and be helpful for wildlife, so early spring is a good time. They

---

PLANTS FOR SEVERE PRUNING

Most species of these genera will tolerate hard pruning (for details *see* page . . .). Some can be maintained routinely this way by pruning to live buds low down on the previous year's growth.

Abelia	*Mahonia*
Artemisia *	*Olearia*
Berberis	*Perovskia* *
Buddleja (B. davidii *)	*Phlomis*
Buxus	*Photinia*
Choisya	*Phygelius* *
Elaeagnus	*Physocarpus*
Erica arborea	*Prunus*
Escallonia	*Pyracantha*
Eucalyptus *	*Rosa*
Griselinia	*Sambucus* *
Hypericum	*Santolina* *
Indigofera *	*Tamarix*
Lavatera *	*(T. ramosissima* *)
Ligustrum	*Taxus*
Lonicera	

* = Plants suited to a routine of annual hard pruning

Easy gardening – the purple smoke bush gets cut back with the grasses in early spring. Then they all grow back sturdily with no watering required.

provide excellent fibrous material for compost making, along with sappy stuff like grass clippings and weeds.

Mature specimens of some trees and shrubs will usually produce new shoots from low down when pruned hard before new growth starts in spring. There may well be more shoots than you want though, in which case some would need to be nipped in the bud *tout de suite*, or at least while still soft enough to break off with the thumb. Select only one strong stem if you want a tree to remain a tree, and be careful not to prune too low down on plants that have been grafted.

Compost-making

Recycling your green waste makes perfect sense. It yields free compost as well as great pleasure from being involved in the natural cycles of growth and decay that support the garden. The time, space, and energy required are well worthwhile if you have them and, as is the case with the raw material, the more you put in the more you get out.

A bit more than half the waste should be fibrous stuff like autumn leaves, dry stems and shrub prunings. Larger woodier pieces could go through a shredder first. The remainder is soft, such as young weeds, grass clippings and raw vegetable kitchen waste. The larger the total volume, the quicker the process, because more heat is generated. Bins of various sorts help keep the heat in, and moisture as well, lessening the need for extra water.

But if you want good crumbly compost in just a few months, your active engagement is crucial. It's an aerobic exercise, for both you and the compost. The energy you put in to turning the heap from time to time, blows oxygen in to energize microbes into a heated frenzy of decomposition. It probably won't get warm enough though to kill all the baddies, so be sure to avoid diseased material, the seeds of weeds and their roots and rhizomes. Pass them on to municipal recyclers who have big stirring machines and volume enough to cook them to death.

There are easier ways if the garden gym sessions don't suit. Anaerobic composting is what happens if the heap is too moist and sloppy with grass clippings, and doesn't get stirred. It's a slower smellier process but gets there in the end. Autumn leaves also take a fair while to break down, so if you've

got lots, they are best kept out of the main compost bin. Shove them damp into black plastic bags pierced with holes, and place in cool shady spot. They will be leaf mould, for mulching after one year and for digging in after two.

Trench composting is a good way to prepare for moisture loving vegetables like runner beans. Just dig a trench in autumn to the depth of a spade, half fill it with raw organic material and cover it over with soil. Recall the location when you sow beans in May. Sheet composting is even simpler and the ideal mulch for the less salubrious corners of the garden. Just spread raw material over the surface and let the worms do the rest. The full power of wiggly things can be harnessed through worm composting, but that's a delight for the connoisseur.

There is one other way to make your own organic matter, and that is to sow a green manure such as field beans, mustard or crimson clover. When the young plants have grown up and before they flower, you dig them into the soil where they grew.

You have to be careful with weeds. There are good ones and bad ones when it comes to compost making, and if you're really organized you'll have a bucket for each. It's the creeping perennial ones that go in the bad bucket along with any at all that are flowering or seeding.

It's easy to say, but weeding is definitely one of those things you should keep on top of, and not just if you are a compulsive tidier. Left alone to grow and set seed, the more they spread and compete, both above ground and below it. The deeper and more extensive their underground parts, the greater the disruption you cause trying to dig them out; damaging your plant roots and interfering with uptake of water and nutrients. But there's weeds and there's weeds. Some are quite nice, and some nice plants can get a bit weedy. Anyway, once you've decided it's a weed, into the bucket it goes, and then it's a chance to get mulching.

It's difficult to make enough compost to keep mulching regularly, so you may need to buy in mulching materials, in order to treat every area, to about ankle depth, at least once a year. Quite when you mulch doesn't matter too much, but the soil should be well moistened beneath the surface, and the plants up and visible so they don't get buried. They don't take kindly to compost piled up round

MULCHING MATERIALS

Mulching is one of those really important things in water-efficient gardening. Not only does it help it retain moisture in the soil and control weeds, but it can improve soil structure, provide nutrients and look nice. Your choice of mulch will depend on priorities, but they are all equally effective in holding in water, and any organic mulch will break down eventually into the soil, improving its structure. What looks nice and what doesn't is a matter of choice so cost, as well as value for feeding and weed control, are the main criteria for these rough guidelines.

Material	Nutrient value	Weed control value	Cost	Other comments
Bark mulch	Low	High	High	Coarser grades last longer and are more effective for weed control
Wood chip	Low	High	Medium	Coarser grades last longer and are more effective for weed control. Check it's been composted
Garden compost	Medium	Low	Low	Normally homemade
Municipal green waste	Low	Medium	Medium	From large-scale recycling
Leafmould	Low	Medium	Low	Normally homemade
Manure	High	Low	Low	Needs to be well-rotted. Often weed infested
Mushroom compost	Medium	Medium	Medium	Often quite alkaline
Biodegradable sheet mulches	Low	High	High	Manufactured from e.g. wool and jute
Mineral aggregates	Low	High	High	Don't decompose. Normally laid on a membrane

their necks, particularly those from dry stony places or when their stems are fresh and green. But if it all gets done, weeded and tidied, there's a warm glow in the heart, for a few seconds at least, until you think of something else.

Oh yes! Watering

Last thing at the end of the day is a good time to water because less is lost through evaporation. First thing, next morning, could be even better (*see* page 145) but it would have to be early, before the sun rises high. Evaporation is mainly a problem where the ground is wetted and exposed to the atmosphere, as happens with a sprinkler on a hose pipe. But the golden rule here is to direct the right amount of water straight to the roots of the plants that need it, and if you can do that, very little will be wasted. Planting on terraces or into hollows, installing pots or pipes next to plants and funnels into hanging baskets can all help a lot, but otherwise it's about how you water, how frequently and for how long.

The sprinkler on a hose pipe

This always seems a terrible waste of water, but if you love to have a bit of green grass then you will need to water it sometimes and it can be done sensibly.

A lawn needs enough water to bring the top 15cm (6in) of soil, where the grass roots grow, from being fairly dry back up to field capacity. Measuring it as you would rain, this is typically about 25mm (1in) depth of water, but would be a bit more in clay and perhaps down to 15mm (½in) in sandy soil. Applying that much to an area 25m²/yd² on one occasion would use a little over 600 litres (150 gallons) of water – about the same amount as an average family of four uses in a day. Not just a drop, it's true, but at least you would be using it mindfully, in a calculated way.

The water your sprinkler applies in, say, half an hour can be measured by placing three or four shallow containers, such as tuna cans, in different places under its shower, and averaging the depth they catch. This will give an idea of how long you need to sprinkle, in order to apply that 25 mm (½ in). Sprinkling for that long, once a week from mid summer to autumn, will help keep the greenness, and if you get the same amount in rain, it won't be needed.

A lawn wants to be watered all over, but the water's not needed anywhere else, and you don't want the wetted areas to overlap too much. Thoughtful moving and setting of an adjustable sprinkler works well. You should re-measure the application rate for each setting you need to fit the shape of your lawn and adjust your timing accordingly. There is a little bit of fussing around and checking your watch, but sprinkling beyond the root zone and beyond the lawn edge really is wastage. So too is using a sprinkler that sprays straight up in the air, and using one during windy conditions or the heat of daytime.

Some automated systems which water straight into the ground can be very efficient if operated correctly, achieving the same as a sprinkler on only about half as much water. With drip irrigation you can position tiny drip heads along a ground level pipe, according to the arrangement of your plants. They each dispense a measured amount of water

A lawn this size could be kept green through summer with just a few sprinklings of 600 litres (150gal).

slowly into the soil. Porous rubber pipe is another option, seeping water out into the soil all along its length. Except in very sandy soils, where the pipes and drip heads need to be closer together, water spreads sideways through the soil. If covered with mulch, water wastage is minimal, and with the right filtration, systems like these can be fitted to harvested rain or grey water tanks.

But as with any system, it's the care with which it's used that determines how efficient it is. This is where the 'right amount' of the golden rule applies, ensuring that you give enough water to bring the soil, where the plant roots are, back up to field capacity. Any more than that is wasted, and any much less isn't really enough. With most plants in beds and borders, this means wetting the soil down to about 30cm (12in). But how do you know when you've done that? Though wetness can be assessed with special meters, a 'hands on' approach is usually fine. Checking at that depth, if loamy soils (*see* page 11) are loose and crumbly, then water is needed, but if they form a ball when moulded, it probably isn't. Sand though is always quite crumbly, and clay quite mouldable unless it's baked, so if sandy soil doesn't stick together at all or clay soil doesn't mould to a worm, then take those as signs that it needs watering.

To get a system to apply the right amount of water, wait until you think the soil should be fairly dry. Then turn the water on and keep checking to see how long it takes to wet the soil at the required depth. You can then check occasionally later to see how quickly it dries out, so the timer can be set accordingly. Sandy soils need the most frequent applications, but as a routine, in weeks without rain, on loamy or heavier soils, you're likely to need up to about 4 hours a week from a drip irrigation or porous pipe system under a mulch. So leaving them on for hours on end more frequently than that would be very wasteful.

Using a watering can is one way to be sure you won't waste water, or kill your plants through overwatering. The time and effort involved is a natural control which is why water restrictions may deem it your only option. It's the labour of love though, so can be enjoyed up to a point, but there's a danger of cutting corners, and not giving plants the water they need. A good thorough watering down to the

WATERING NEW PLANTINGS

Whether measuring water in cans, or time spent holding a hose, checking the soil wetness (*see* page 150) can give an idea of the depth it reaches and how quickly it dries. However, the following guidelines should help, and of course if there is no pot or pipe to water into, you must water slowly enough for it to percolate down.

Type/Size	Time interval between waterings or following heavy rain	Amount of water (10 litre cans)	How long this is needed for*
1 small hanging basket plant	1 day	1 teacup	until autumn
Bedding plant from a 9 cm container	5 days	1 litre	1 month
Shrub or perennial from 2–3 litre container	10 days	1 can	2 months
Tree or shrub from a 15-litre container	15 days	2 cans	3 months
Larger tree from a 30-litre container	20 days	4 cans	until autumn

*Watering may well still be necessary after this period, perhaps over another two years for the large tree. It needn't be so frequent and could just be done as required, but more water should be given because of the larger root system that the plant will have.

roots, then a period of drying is better for plants than just being watered little and often. If you only wet the surface, roots don't grow deep and the plant continues to rely on you for its water.

New plantings

This is one kind of watering that everybody with a garden will probably need to do sometimes. Depending on when you plant and the weather, it may not need doing, but all plants should have moist roots when planted. Also, if they are in leaf, one watering at least is a good idea, to settle the soil around their roots.

It's normally only the ones you plant and forget about that really suffer, so one way of dealing with it is to look every day and water at the very first signs of stress (*see* page 128). Another way is to water at particular intervals following the last heavy rain. The smaller the plant, the shorter the intervals but the less water it needs and the quicker it will become established.

Using water wisely

Plants in the wild only get what nature gives them, and most plants we grow can be just as tough. With plants chosen carefully to be at one with their surrounds – the soil, the wildlife and weather – and us not intervening any more than we need to, we can have beautiful gardens, and time to relax. But it's an artificial system that we've assembled, so integral we are, and ultimately responsible for maintaining the peace. Assisting plants with their watery needs will always be part of that job, and part of that too will be making best use of the water we've got.

All this can be made as technical and scientific as you like, but ultimately gardening is about how much you care – the closeness you feel with the plants you grow and the soil you look after. Pumps, meters, timers and drip heads all have their place if you're so inclined, but the spirit of water-efficient gardening lies in the simplicity that gardening is. Plants, a water butt, a few tools, a watering can and some outdoor space are all you really need, and a good feel for those things which are most important when gardening with full regard to water.

Water-Efficient Gardening – The Golden Rules
- Enrich the soil with compost right from the start.
- Choose plants to suit the conditions.
- Use small plants and sow seed as much you can.
- Plant in the dormant season.
- Collect as much rainwater as you can.
- Get the right amount of water to the roots of plants that need it.
- More compost, or similar material, used as a mulch.

Glossary

Anti-transpirant sprays
Waxy materials that can be sprayed onto the leaves of plants to temporarily reduce transpiration.

Artificial windbreaks
Various plastic sheet materials that can be erected to form a vertical barrier between plants and the prevailing wind. They have to be permeable so as not to resist the wind, but to allow it to pass through slowly.

Available water capacity
The amount of water in a soil between its field capacity and its wilting point. This is the water a plant can extract.

Balance
A principle of garden design concerned with ensuring that features on each side of a view are similar in their visual impact. Whether arranged symmetrically or not, they should still appear balanced.

Baseline
A term used in surveying for a line along which measurements are taken. In measuring home gardens, the baselines are usually extensions from the house.

Bedding plants
Plants that are planted out into beds for seasonal display.

Biological control
The control of pests by introducing or encouraging other organisms that are predators or parasites of those pests.

Biome
A distinct natural community of plants and animals that occurs over major geographical regions throughout the globe. Biomes are characterized by their dominant vegetation and prevailing climate.

Capping
A problem with structure at the soil surface when the lumps disintegrate after heavy rain or watering. As the surface then dries, it forms a hard crust that can obstruct the germination of seeds.

Crop rotation
A system of growing vegetables whereby different types of crops, e.g. root crops, brassicas and legumes, are grown in a different patch of ground each year. It prevents the build-up of pests and diseases and helps keep the ground fertile.

Cultural control
The use of good gardening practice as a means of controlling pests, diseases and weeds. Choosing plants to suit the growing conditions is the starting point for cultural control.

Cytoplasm
The jelly-like material, comprised mainly of water, in which the living processes take place in plant cells.

Division of space
The use of elements such as walls or plantings that rise above eye level and so create separate spaces in a garden.

Drifts
Groups of plants deliberately arranged to form irregular flowing shapes through a bed or border.

Drip irrigation
A system of watering where plastic tubing, placed close to the roots of a plant, applies water slowly at low pressure. It is sometimes called trickle irrigation.

Dwarfing rootstocks
These are used on most fruit trees you can get for gardens. The trees are propagated by grafting them onto these rootstocks, which then restrict their growth, making them more compact and easier to care for.

Exotic plants
Plants that originate in other countries. This term is also used in referring to plants with a particularly 'exotic' look, such as palms and bamboos.

Extensions from a building
A method of surveying whereby the lines of a building are extended outwards for measuring. Because the building is right-angular, and so can be drawn accurately, it makes an effective starting point for an accurate drawing.

Field capacity
The amount of water a soil can hold without any draining away.

Focalization
A principle of garden design where use is made of focal features, such as sculptures, or distinctive-looking plants, to draw the attention of a garden viewer.

Frost pocket
A low-lying area where cold air accumulates, making frost more likely to occur.

Glyphosate
The active ingredient of a range of herbicides, which are effective in killing most perennial weeds.

Green manures
Crops that are grown so that they can be dug into the ground to improve the soil. Used in places that would otherwise be fallow, they also help to hold nutrients in the soil and protect the surface from heavy rain.

Growing hard
A term applied to growing plants with minimal care. It relies heavily on choosing plants to suit the growing conditions.

Hardy plants
Plants that can survive outside all-year-round in a particular area.

Humus
Organic matter in the latter stages of decomposition, when the leaves and twigs, etc. are no longer recognizable.

Hydrophytes
Plants that are naturally adapted to growing in very wet conditions.

John Innes
The name of a range of composts for potting and propagation. Their distinctive feature is that they contain loam, unlike most other composts you can buy.

Liming
The application of lime to the soil. It is normally applied in the form of ground limestone or hydrated lime.

Loam
A type of soil texture where sand, silt and clay occur in fairly even proportions. The term also refers to the soil contained in John Innes composts.

Membrane
A term used for certain fabrics that can be laid on the ground as sheet mulches.

Mulch
A material that is spread on the surface of the ground between plants. It may be a loose organic or mineral material, or can be a sheet material of some kind.

Mycorrhizae
Natural associations between fungi and the roots of some plants whereby each benefits from the other. In some soils the necessary fungi are not present, so plants may be benefit from having them added.

Native plants
Plants that naturally occur in a particular area and were not introduced there by people.

Natural habitats
The conditions in which plants naturally grow in the wild. They are typically defined by the soil, microclimate or type of vegetation that prevails.

Nitrogen
One of the major nutrients needed by plants. It encourages green leafy growth.

Offset
A term used in surveying for plotting a single point by taking a measurement from it at a right-angle to a baseline, i.e. the shortest distance from the point to the baseline. The point is then plotted on paper by placing a set square on the baseline.

Osmosis
This is how plants take up water. The soil water, being more dilute than the water in plants, passes into the root through the semi-permeable membrane of the root hairs. If the soil is contaminated, for example by salt, water may instead pass out of the plant.

Panning
A problem with structure beneath the soil surface, whereby an impermeable layer develops that can obstruct root growth and the downward movement of water.

Pesticides
Chemicals that are used to control pests, or more generally, any garden chemical used for pest, disease or weed control.

Phosphorus
One of the major nutrients that plants need. It has a particular role in encouraging root growth.

Photosynthesis
The process by which plants make their own food using sunlight, carbon dioxide and water. It can be obstructed by drought, when plants close their stomata to reduce transpiration, and so lose the ability to take in carbon dioxide.

Piped drainage system
A system of pipes that collect rainfall from the soil and carry it away to some kind of outfall, e.g. a ditch or a soakaway.

Physical control
The physical removal of pests, diseases and weeds, e.g. picking off caterpillars or removing infected stems.

Potager
A garden that combines food production with ornamental display.

Potassium
One of the major nutrients that plants need. It encourages flowering and fruiting and makes plants more resistant to diseases and stresses like cold and drought.

Proportion and scale
Principles of design concerned with achieving pleasing size relationships between elements of a garden.

Rain garden
A sunken bed that receives water run-off from an adjacent hard surface. Ideal for moisture-loving plants, it also reduces storm water problems by filtering the run-off and allowing its slow percolation down into the water table.

Rain shadow
A piece of ground that is sheltered from prevailing winds and the rainfall that they carry.

Resistant varieties
Cultivars of plants which have an in-built resistance to particular pests or diseases.

Respiration
The process by which plants break down sugar to release the energy they need. It requires a warm temperature and a supply of oxygen, so doesn't happen properly in compacted or saturated soil.

Rhythm
A principle of garden design concerned with creating a sense of movement whereby the eye is drawn through the garden. Flowing lines in the layout may achieve this, or the repetition of a particular shape in the plants or sculpture.

RHS
Royal Horticultural Society. The most important organization for gardening in the UK.

Root hairs
Slender extensions from just behind the tips of young growing roots. They are really important for taking up water, so when roots are disturbed through transplanting, the plant is disadvantaged until it grows new ones.

Running measurements
A term used in surveying for measurements taken along a baseline. They are taken accumulatively, so that the baseline starts at 0, and each subsequent measurement adds to that, e.g. 3, 7 and finally 10, along a 10m line.

Sap vacuole
The large cavity in many plant cells that contains a dilute solution of sugars, salts and other solutes dissolved in water.

Saturation point
This is when all of the pore spaces in the soil are full of water.

Scale plan
A plan drawing with the correct dimensions of length and breadth shown at a smaller scale than they really are. At scale 1 in 100, 1m on the ground is drawn as 1cm. At 1 in 50, 1m is drawn as 2cm and at 1 in 200, it is 5mm.

Seasonal plantings
Short-term plantings for display in particular seasons. When the display is finished, the plants are replaced.

Sepals
The individual segments that make up the outer whorl of a flower. They are typically green and protect the flower before it opens.

Soakaway
A hole dug in the ground and filled with free-draining materials, such as bricks and stones, through which water can percolate away from the surface.

Soil structure
The way the sand, silt and clay particles in the soil are joined together into lumps.

Soil texture
This is to do with how sandy, silty or clayey a soil is.

Stamens
The individual male reproductive structures in a flower. Their role is to produce and release pollen.

Stomata
Tiny pores, mainly on the under-surface of leaves, through which water vapour is lost in the process of transpiration, and CO_2 enters for photosynthesis. When a plant senses drought, it can rapidly close its stomata to conserve water.

Surface compaction
A problem with structure, common in clay soils, where particles at the soil surface become compacted together by being worked or walked on when wet.

Topiary
The trimming of plants, such as box or yew, into artificial shapes.

Transpiration
The loss of water vapour from leaves, encouraged by extreme high temperatures, dry air and wind. It can put plants under stress, but is also important for cooling, and for drawing nutrients up the plant.

Water reservoirs
An in-built vessel at the bottom of a hanging basket that holds onto water. A disc of polythene, or a small saucer, could be placed inside the liner of a wire basket to give a similar effect.

Water retaining gels
Products that can be mixed into soil or composts to increase the amount of water they can hold. They are usually synthetic materials that swell when they're wetted.

Water table
A term loosely used for the zone, down underground, where the soil is saturated with water. More correctly, the 'table' is the top of this zone.

Wetting agent
A product that can be sprayed onto lawns in order to improve their ability to allow percolation of water down into the soil where the grass roots are.

Wild plants
Plants which reproduce to form natural populations in a particular area, whether they're native or originally introduced by people.

Wilting point
The relatively small amount of water that plants can't extract because it is held in the soil so tightly.

Xerophytes
Plants which are naturally adapted to growing in very dry conditions.

Further reading

BOOKS

Adams, C.R., Bamford, K.M., and Early, M.P. *Principles of Horticulture* (Butterworth Heinemann, 2008) (A good guide to soil science, plant science and plant health.)

Bennett, Jennifer *Dryland Gardening: plants that survive and thrive in tough conditions* (Firefly Books, 2005) (More ideas, and some different plants from across the Atlantic.)

Chatto, Beth *Beth Chatto's Gravel Garden* (Frances Lincoln, 2000) (A classic book about a superb dry garden.)

Cooke, Ian *Waterwise Gardening* (New Holland Publishers Ltd, 2008) (Another gardener's perspective on the same subject as this.)

Lancaster, Roy *Plants for Places* (Dorling Kindersley: RHS books, 2001) (This is one of a range of really useful books produced by the RHS. Others include the Encyclopedias of *Gardening*, *Garden Design* and *Garden Plants*.)

WEBSITES

www.rhs.org.uk – an enormous resource for gardening information including lots on this topic and the excellent Plant Finder facility.

www.waterwise.org.uk – this includes details of outdoor products that have been awarded the Waterwise Marque for their special value in water-efficiency.

www.southernwater.co.uk – this contains a guide to choosing drought-resistant plants for a range of soils and conditions.

www.pfaf.org – a database of useful plants with information on cultivation requirements (including drought-resistance) and their natural habitats.

www.davesgarden.com – a networking site for gardeners to share their experiences of growing plants.

Index